THE
DISBELIEVER'S
DICTIONARY

GARFINKLE ESTATE

A GLEEFULLY DISRESPECTFUL
LEXICON OF CANADA TODAY

BRIAN FAWCETT

SOMERVILLE HOUSE PUBLISHING

TORONTO

Copyright © 1997 by Brian Fawcett

All rights reserved. No part of this publication may be
reproduced or transmitted in any form or by any means—
electronic or mechanical, including photocopy, recording
or any information storage and retrieval system—without
written permission from the Publisher, except by a reviewer
who wishes to quote brief passages for inclusion in a review.

Canadian Cataloguing in Publication Data

Fawcett, Brian, 1944–
     The disbeliever's dictionary: a gleefully disrespectful
     lexicon of Canada today

ISBN 1-894042-10-7

1. Canada – Politics and government – 1993–   –Humor.*
I. Title.

FC173.F38 1997   971.064'8'0207   C97-932182-4
F1026.4.F38 1997

Book design: Gordon Robertson
Printed in Canada

Published by Somerville House Publishing
a division of Somerville House Books Limited
3080 Yonge Street, Suite 5000, Toronto, Ontario M4N 3N1
Website: www.sombooks.com
E-mail: sombooks@goodmedia.com

Somerville House Publishing acknowledges the financial
assistance of the Ontario Arts Council, the Ontario Development Corporation, and the Department of Communications.

Acknowledgments

Leanna Crouch, Nora Abercrombie, Judith Rudikoff, Janice Zawerbny all read versions of the dictionary and offered invaluable editorial and conceptual help. Stan Persky, despite his misgivings about the project, did an 11th hour line-by-liner on the manuscript that broadened its scope, put some needed limits on my sense of fun and curbed my tendency to read conspiracy where there is merely opaque confusion and the mechanical chaos of systems grounded in binary logic. Patrick Crean, my editor, guided this project through difficulties that sometimes blotted out the sun with their sheer volume and cloudiness. Finally, I need to thank Graziano Marchese of Dooney's Café, Toronto, who had to take on a multinational corporation to continue providing me with office space, good cheer and drinkable coffee.

Introduction

A few years ago the Vancouver Writers' Festival dragooned me and several other writers into a panel discussion about writing and politics. At the time, such panels were the arts community's way of convincing itself it was responding to the then-barely evident corporate program to replace civility, culture and politics with entrepreneurial aggression, personal finances and economics. But while our panel dutifully and sententiously prattled along, full of itself and post-modernist deconstructive theory-with-a-capital-T nonsense, a middle-aged woman in the audience decided she couldn't stand us any longer. "I want to know," she finger-pointed right at me, "what makes *you* proud of being a Canadian?"

"What makes me proud of being a Canadian?" I echoed. "That I don't have to be proud of being a Canadian." My reply drew a good-natured Canadian laugh from the audience, and we went back to our semantic ditherings, cheered but not quite enlightened.

We might have been enlightened if we'd stopped to think about how accurate a description my quick answer offered. Canadians have never had to live with imperial pride, we haven't had to suffer through compulsory flag-waving jingoism, we're not compelled, by law or sense of obligation, to learn the dubious art of brandishing automatic rifles at all those foreigners who don't believe that our country is on a special mission from God. We're defined, in large degree, by our relative freedom as perpetrators or victims, from nearly all of the defining cruelties, injustices and stupidities of the 20th Century. It is the things we *haven't* been subjected to that define us.

We've been a country without the sort of grandiose mission that makes people in other countries crazy and violent, but that doesn't mean Canada hasn't had a purpose. In fact, it has had an exquisitely elegant one since the 1790s: to keep Canadians from having to be Americans. From the start, we have been what we are not.

That may not be good enough much longer, and that is what occasions this dictionary. It's not just because GATT and the World Bank are now demanding we conform to their conventions. There's a deeper uneasiness that the institutions we grew up trusting are now lying systematically to us: the government, the businesses that sell us what we need to live, and the corporations that now control most of the important instruments of living, and which determine, despite denials, if there are going to be any occupations for us to make decent lives with. It may be the Information Age we're living in, but that has turned out to mean that once we've crawled out from under the deluge of irrelevant data, we have to plough through its disinformation, misinformation and plain old lies, bullshit and nonsense to discover what our surroundings and ourselves have come to.

Now, sure as hell, business-like optimists will call this negativity and yammer on about unleashing the Entrepreneurial

Spirit, Getting With the Program, Going with the Flow, and before we know it we'll be knee-deep in a lot of half-assed nonsense about the Triumph of Capitalism, Survival of the Fittest and other upper case glamourizations of dogs eating dogs.

I'm an optimist myself, but not about the same things. Canadians, for instance, don't spend their waking hours fending off hostile clans with automatic weapons nor do we have to dodge artillery shells or machete strokes because our ancestors called themselves one thing and not another. Canadians are decent, polite, not particularly God-fearing people who watch *Hockey Night in Canada* as an act of patriotism. We drink beer that has enough alcohol in it to get us drunk, and we treat the poor, sick and elderly with a degree of generosity. Shouldn't we be celebrating our relatively generous and peaceful multiplicity, not trying to crawl over one another's backs or incite one another to violence by scraping at our differences until they bleed?

In case I sound like another grumpy adult telling you to eat your peas because people are starving in Asia, let me put this another way. In a country as complicated as Canada has always been, the sort of yes/no east/west Canada/Quebec thinking everyone is slipping into has a dangerous and not very distant terminal point: you line up everything and everyone on one side or the other, choose your side and commence the drift to a Final Solution.

My solution? Governments that treat people decently and are willing to make decisions on behalf of the people who elected them. For that we need conscious, knowledgeable citizens who recognize the *private* obligation to treat one another decently. There may be some sort of moral absolute lurking somewhere in this, but there's a more important common sense. Competition is a fine thing in relevant doses, but cruelty and class warfare have never worked.

This dictionary is the long form to the answer to the question that woman in Vancouver asked me years ago. It records the things I'm proud of, the things I'm not proud of, and it's pretty exhaustive about what threatens our historical privilege of not having to be self-conscious of our pride. Throughout, I've defended just one political principle: the right to be impertinent, insolent and irreverent in the face of any and every authority. This right is the one—the only one—that guarantees freedom of expression and a minimum degree of public discourse and social justice. Take it away—or fail to exercise it—and democracy retreats.

I don't claim that I've assembled an array of indisputable facts here, only that I've tried to see my country and its condition without flinching from the duty to offer nothing and no one unexamined respect—or freedom from the possibility of a wisecrack. If we're going to succeed in living together—Quebec, Ontario, B.C. and the rest—without turning into the squabbling confederacy of blow-hard tribalized axe murderers our current leaders are drawing us toward, the average citizen is going to have to operate with more definitions that penetrate the soft lies that are smothering us with a toxic glue made up partly of gleaming but pointless product and partly our own goofiness and greed.

Toronto, July 6, 1997

THE DISBELIEVER'S DICTIONARY

ABORTION

In R. v. Morgentaler (1988)—the last intelligent Canadian Supreme Court decision before the institution fell hostage to political correctness—Canada decided that it could live without abortion laws, on the constitutional ground that there is a class of important personal decisions in which the state ought not to interfere. Despite predictions that the country would fall into social chaos at the hands of hordes of fetus-murdering Medeas, the Canadian family continues to wobble along without notable damage other than the incitements caused by shopping malls, TV and the Internet. A few hardy souls claiming direct access to God continue to loiter outside the bubble zones of the few clinics courageous enough to provide this medical service. See *Obscenity*

ACCOUNTABILITY

A substance that no longer exists in Canada's post-accountable financial sector. When it finally comes time for everyone to add two and two, don't be surprised if all those owners of late-model Lexus and Mercedes-Benz automobiles panic at the mention of "accountability".

ACID RAIN

The response to this crisis is a longstanding Canadian version of dithering-while-Rome-burns. In this case, it's our forests dissolving from airborne sulfuric acid, and our lakes dying because the water is too acidic to support complex biological systems. Acid rain is a currently unfashionable but solvable problem. It hasn't been taken seriously because both our governments and our industrial chiefs believe that the general public hasn't got the attention span of a milk cow. The result has been a twenty-year multigovernment Alphonse & Gaston jamboree so dumb it wouldn't even get a laugh in a milking barn.

BRYAN ADAMS

Gravel-voiced androgynous Vancouver musician distinguished by his ability to discover and cover the musical equivalent of dead neutral. Adams illustrates what Canadian culture will be like if it becomes wholly defined by the marketplace: Joe Cocker without drugs, alcohol or demons, management by middle-aged guys who think lunch with Tina Turner is a religious experience, rock 'n' roll for chartered accountants and mutual fund managers. It promises a vast middle ground swept by violins and a soporific base that stretches from our fingertips to eternity but is without profound highs or lows.

ADANAC

Most Canadian cities have streets and business firms named Adanac. Bet you won't find a *Setats Detinu* Drive in the U.S. or a *Rue de Ecnarf* in France. Is a country that resorts to spelling its name backwards in order to provide sufficient appellations for thoroughfares and corporations suffering from terminal poverty of imagination or a national learning disability?

AGGRIEVED WHITE GUYS

A group of generally well-heeled, expensively educated but physically awkward males who work in or close to the mass media, sometimes having been placed there by wealthy parents or mentors. They are often characterized by facial fat and the belief that they are victims of a conspiracy of black and Asian women, homosexuals, communists and other marginalized yet mysteriously powerful minorities able to take over the government and prevent aggrieved white guys and their families from experiencing the world the way it was forty years ago. It's tempting to dismiss them as a uniquely Canadian version of Revenge of the Nerds, but their aggressive rancour and their influence argue for other responses. See *Conservative Intellectuals, Doug Collins, Michael Coren, Andrew Coyne, Mike Duffy, David Frum, Vaughn Palmer, Michael Walker*

AIRBORNE

Disgraced regiment that lurched so far out of control during a brief assignment in Somalia in 1991 that the government was forced to disband it. No one had the courage to cashier its members, and they've been dispersed to infect the rest of the armed forces.

AIRBUSES

Recent vintage passenger jets purchased by Air Canada from a Euro consortium, supposedly to offset the giveaway of other Canadian aerospace assets to U.S. companies. Their planes tend to rattle while in flight because their parts are fabricated in six different countries and therefore don't quite fit together, and they've been known to run out of fuel in awkward situations. Airbuses, it seems, may also cause embarrassing Swiss bank accounts and Caribbean recreational properties to appear in the hands of Canadian politicians and their advisors.

AIRLINES
In the early 1980s, Canada had four functioning Canadian-owned airlines, one publicly owned, and a raft of independent charter and regional carriers. Then the industry was *deregulated*, supposedly to foster competition, cheapen fares and open up the marketplace. Result? Two major air carriers, both virtual subsidiaries of larger American air carriers. Meanwhile, the two majors have gobbled up 90 percent of regional carriers, so that it's now difficult to get on a plane in Canada that isn't controlled by offshore profit vampires. Hey! What happened to the cheap fares and the competition? And what do "deregulation" and "open up the marketplace" *really* mean?

ALBERTA
Former oil-rich sector of Prairies where citizens don't believe in taxation, foreigners or any other part of Canada except Texas and Montana. Albertans think consciousness-raising is a matter of slapping people across the side of the head with the Bible, subjecting them to motivational speeches by blow-hard former Alberta premiers, their sons and/or former radio talk-show hosts, and preparing them for the eventual war between the city-states of Edmonton and Calgary.

AMERICANS

Most Canadians believe that Americans are friendlier, wealthier, smarter and less subject to taxation. In fact, only American *tourists* and a few celebrities regularly seen dining in Los Angeles and New York restaurants are wealthier than the average Canadian. In their own country, Americans are victims of exponentially higher crime rates, less civilized social security, no visible health care and are being squeezed as brutally by multilateral corporate trade agreements as the average Canadian. Americans tend to admire Canadian institutions, but worry about possible communistic origins. Americans who *really* admire Canadian institutions, mores and ways of life tend to emigrate to Canada and become almost the only Canadians who give a damn about protecting our institutions, mores and ways of life. See *Murkans, Amer-Canadians*

AMER-CANADIANS

The reason why this term is unfamiliar is that U.S. immigrants to Canada are about the only immigrants we have willing to be unhyphenated citizens.

BARBARA AMIEL

She's a former journalist now armed with a phony Brit accent, a very wealthy husband and the most shrill political rhetoric this side of Diane Francis. She also appears to be the only member of the conservative intelligentsia who has a sense of humour, and among the few who display any sensible delight at exercising wealth and power.

ANIK
Canadian-owned communications satellites reputed to be in the sky over our heads at all times. Canadian communications satellites have a tendency to go off-line whenever new channel applications are before the CRTC.

PAUL ANKA
First human to repeat the phrase "I'm so young and you're so old" without worrying about getting a clout across the side of the head. He has now done it 30,000 times in public. Anka supposedly grew up in Ottawa, then moved to Las Vegas, where he grew bald, older and difficult to distinguish physically from Wayne Newton, Moses Znaimer and several dozen Mafia captains currently under indictment. Believed by a solid majority of middle-aged and elderly RV owners in Eastern Ontario to be a Canadian national treasure.

ANNE OF AVONLEA
PEI's most lucrative export, a national treasure or a lesbian costume/soap opera, depending on which washroom walls you're reading or defacing. Key Canadian export to Japan.

APEC
Asia-Pacific Economic Cooperation forum, an eight-year-old quasi-government think-tank dedicated to compulsory tariff-free trade and other globalist favourites. APEC conference delegates and organization officials consciously represent "economies" rather than "countries". Don't confuse this organization with the Association for the Preservation of the English Language in

Canada, (a far-right anti-Quebec offshoot of the already-far-right NCC) which is now locked deep in the Reform Party's closet, or with OPEC, the original "let's exploit everyone" cartel. Sensible folks should beware of all three organizations about equally.

ARMED FORCES

Vestigial and highly antiquated body no one had the courage to remainder after WW II and which no government now has sufficient will to put a leash on. Before and during WW II, Canadian armed forces were treated alternately as lab and wharf rats by the Allied High Command, sent on suicidal raids and quartered in the worst available conditions to keep them away from British women. The current CAF are exclusively drawn from rural populations in Alberta, Quebec and Newfoundland, a demographic which might leave Canada without any armed forces if things go badly for federalists in the next few years. Is that a problem or not?

AVRO ARROW

The Arrow was an all-Canadian state-of-the-art fighter plane cancelled in 1959 when John Diefenbaker, faced by U.S. diplomatic pressures to allow U.S. missiles onto Canadian soil, not only blinked, but rolled over. Canada has been an American military satellite since.

ASSURANCES

Free trade code word moaned frequently during Free Trade negotiations by Canadian negotiators. Freely translated, it seems to have meant "hump me hard". The American response to this was typical, and a simple translation reads: "Of course I'll respect you afterward. . . ."

MARGARET ATWOOD

Canada's best-known writer has a big brain and an unerring sense of what guys are playing with in their pockets. For reasons unknown, she's become the first public figure ambitious assholes attack when decrying Canadian culture. When she was younger, she gave a credible impersonation of Miss Piggy when buzzed by fools. More serene now, she merely writes decent novels filled with lucid if conventional English sentences and exudes acid-laced common sense in the face of incoming lunacies of all sorts. These are unfair questions to ask, but is Atwood a greater writer than, say, South Africa's Nadine Gordimer? What kind and quality of novels would she have written had she been born a white South African, a Czech, or simply twenty years later than she was?

AUGUST 1

Recently invented Bank holiday (it seems to have replaced the November 11th Armistice Day observances but no government official will admit that). Having a holiday in August is an illustration of our newfound social pragmatism. There's no occasion for an August 1st holiday except that the weather is good and the tourism industry campaigned hard for it. And there's nothing to celebrate in early August, except maybe the suntans Health Canada says we're not supposed to have.

THE AUTO PACT

Supposedly a trade pact that blew up on the Americans, it is actually a function of monetary policy, or was until Brian Mulroney pegged the Canadian dollar artificially high and caused an exodus of auto manufacturing to Ohio and anywhere else in the U.S. and Mexico where the incest rate is abnormally high and wages are low. The auto pact still exists, mainly as a tribute to the power of inertia.

AWARDS GALAS AND DINNERS

The Canadian media and business communities in the 1990s have become as vulgar and as crazed as Americans are when it comes to shameless self-congratulation and self-promotion of its achievers and celebrities. Whether this is a subschedule of the 1988 and 1993 trade agreements isn't clear. While Canadian media award galas are used as occasions to suck up to (and subsequently ignore) the multicultural community, business award ceremonies are generally occasions to reassert that aging white guys are still firmly in control. The relative degrees of insincerity and jibberish in both kinds of galas are indistinguishably total. See *Genies, Junos, Geminis*

LLOYD AXWORTHY

Superbland federal Liberal MP and lone star of the West not to be confused with Pierre Trudeau's former body-shield Tom Axworthy. Lloyd was supposed to be the guardian of the Canadian social net in the post-Mulroney era. But because Axworthy couldn't stare down Paul Martin, Jr. and his herd of deficit-crazed closet New Conservatives in the Chrétien government cabinet, the post-Mulroney era hasn't begun. Axworthy remains living proof that alphabetical order of surnames is a key to electoral but not political success.

DONOVAN BAILEY

Speeder, Oakville homeboy, beauty—and a welcome relief from Ben and other Johnsons. He may or may not be the fastest man in the world but at worst he's only a part-time jerk as a public figure and role model, and then mostly right after he's won a race.

BALLERINAS

While they're youthful, ballerinas are anorexic women with long, elegant necks and bleeding feet. After age thirty-five, they're aging neurotics, fading beauties, fronts for Arts lobbies or walking cocktail circuit prizes (these categories are *not* exclusive of one another). See *Karen Kain, Gisella Witkowsky, Veronica Tennant*

BANANAS

Code word for current tendency of Canadian economic, political and cultural goals to emulate those in Banana-growing areas of Central and South America: the dispersal of taxation monies to multinationals willing to pretend they'll employ indigenous workers, an end to government taxation powers, and the extermination of any and all government services, Crown corporations, public monopolies—along with any citizens whose activities tend to impinge on the tax-free incomes of high-income citizens and/or corporations. During the 1990s, our political system has been largely reshaped to achieve these ends, but

Canadians remain oblivious to the consequent influx of tarantulas or the poverty that comes with economic systems based on banana cultivation and export.

CANADA'S DUMBEST BANDS

Crash Test Dummies, Möxie Fruvous, Moist, Barenaked Ladies. Historically: Glass Tiger, Loverboy, Rush, and any group (musical or not) associated with Burton Cummings.

CHARTERED BANKS

Until deregulation, banking in Canada was done through five major Chartered Banks and a smaller tier of credit unions and trust companies that tried, officially at least, to be sensitive to local conditions. Most of the small credit unions have been swallowed by larger ones, the trust companies are either bankrupt or owned by larger financial corporations, the Chartered Banks are on every street corner with their jaws open for business, and now there's a tier of tower-owning offshore banks in the major cities that never seem to have any physical customers and are presumably here to oversee and extend our foreign debt. All financial institutions are now outrageously profitable and uniformly inhospitable to the small businesses they spend millions convincing us they're really there to help, with the original chartered banks leading the way.

BARENAKED LADIES

When these words come to mean a group of self-consciously cute, pudgy male musicians from Toronto dressed up with sideburns and short pants who appear to be bosom friends of Rita MacNeil, you know the country is in trouble.

BATON BROADCASTING

Now run by ex-CBC majordomo Ivan Fecan, and owned by nice common folks named Eaton and Bassett, Baton is trying to be a convincing argument that private sector television can replace the CBC. It's hard to say if what ails the CBC is infectious, but when Baton picked up Rita MacNeil after the CBC couldn't afford her snack budget, a strong piece of evidence was offered.

BCNI

Business Council on National Issues. Right wing lobby from hell, and a *de facto* shadow government with a deep suntan. Former Mexican President Carlos Salinas would feel comfortable at one of their strategy sessions. See NAPO

PERRIN BEATTY

Premier upper class twit of the 1980s, former Mulroney cabinet minister designated by Jean Chrétien to finish the destruction of the CBC begun by Marcel Masse. Sleeps in bunny-footed sleepers.

JEANNE BEKER

Host of Znaimer-produced *Fashion Television*. There are 150 million people across the world who recognize Beker—and don't recognize that she's Canadian. Canadians who've seen her merely try to figure out if it's the Joker or Penguin from *Batman* she resembles. And who started that nasty rumour about her relationship with Sting, anyway?

RALPH BENMERGUI

A few years ago, this man, together with terminally earnest Tina Srebotnjak, was CBC management's idea of television intellectualism. But he has since plummeted from the middlebrow haven of *Midday* to the ill-conceived and misnomered *Ralph Benmergui Live* all the way down to hosting an unresearched CBC Newsworld open mouth show from the corporation's rotunda in Toronto. Benmergui still fancies himself a comedian, and commentators and critics across the country still stay up late at night trying to think of ways to convince him he's not.

AVIE BENNETT

Toronto real estate magnate who rescued McClelland & Stewart from Jack McClelland and has pumped about $2 million annually into the company ever since because he believes in the value of independent culture and the virtue of arm's length cultural management. No one in the history of this country's publishing industry has done anything as generous, and no one has received less of the recognition deserved. Bennett is the best argument going for local/private control of cultural assets, which is the only argument over culture no one has been making, even though it's the only sane one. It's too bad we don't deserve Bennett, and a tragedy that he's the only one we have.

PAUL BERNARDO

Canada's celebrity criminal for the 1990s. He got his *modus operandi* from reading business books and watching inspirational business movies like *Wall Street*, and is, minus the gory killings, exactly the kind of human being that the New Conservative

revolution glorifies: an entrepreneur who takes what he wants
and damn the bleeding hearts. During his trial, there was about
50 percent less screwing going on between married Canadian
couples, and handiCam sales dropped across the country.
About the only nice thing to be said about Bernardo is that he
helped Canadians recognize the superiority of the Canadian
judicial system over that of the United States. He's unlikely to
survive very long in jail, which won't bring many Canadians to
tears.

PIERRE BERTON

Polyester *aficionado*, Anglican historian, television panelist and
charter member of Toronto's legendary and probably fictitious
Swordsmen's Club, an antediluvian misogynist group that its
surviving members are trying to forget. Since Berton is also a
genuine cultural treasure, his excesses, along with his taste in
leisure suits, are forgivable even though it'll be well into the next
century before there will be Toronto literary parties where you
won't hear someone snickering about either the dullness of the
swords or the colour of Berton's suits.

BICULTURALISM

With growing suspicion inside Quebec that French Canadians
weren't getting enough jobs as federal civil servants, the Canadian government designated Canada a bilingual and bicultural
nation in 1971 after an eight year Royal Commission. The Commission conducted its deliberations in both French and English,
which limited membership to bilingual Anglos living within a
ten mile radius of Ottawa and, in its last years, to friends of Pierre

Trudeau or his philosopher corps. Québécois radicals branded the Royal Commission's report Anglo window dressing while they filled out the job applications. Western Canadians were infuriated because they could only understand half of what was being said and assumed, with a small degree of justification, that the real stuff was being said in French by and to Quebec. A quarter century later bilingualism has given the Québécois 90 percent of federal civil service jobs, and Canadians are now regularly treated to the comedy of Anglo politicians choking the airwaves with the most dreadful pidgin French spoken anywhere in the world.

To stuff a gag into the mouths of other instantly whining ethnicities, Trudeau appointed a minister for multiculturalism in 1972, even though no official policy was adopted until 1987. Biculturalism was effectively replaced by multiculturalism by the early 1980s in the minds of everyone except rednecks in Alberta and Quebec's separatists, both of whom began a Long March-style campaign to replace the linguistic elements of both bi and multiculturalism with Texas Oilman Chinook and near-French commercial joual, respectively, and to supplant culture of any kind with life-style accoutrements of *laissez-faire* capitalism. Other constituencies in the country remain more tolerant and generous, despite the Reform Party.

BIG GOVERNMENT

Favoured corporate sector stalking horse in the 1990s trotted out whenever business boffins need to cover up their own screw-ups and inefficiencies. Never mind that government program spending as a percentage of GNP is well below 1967 levels, or that a quick glance at any big-city skyline will tell you which sector has gotten big in the last thirty years, and where the "big" problem now lies. In the late 1990s, the target of the corporations has been broadened from "big government" to demonize all government. As economics subsumes politics, government itself has become the designated enemy for the globalists.

ROBIN BLASER

If you want to know what it is to carry on a passionate lifelong artistic project that doesn't abrogate the rules of discourse and scholarship, find and read *The Holy Forest*, the magnum opus of this Idaho-raised now-septuagenarian Vancouver poet, teacher and scholar. Blaser immigrated to Canada in 1965 and for a quarter of a century taught an entire generation of young Canadian intellectuals and writers at Simon Fraser University how to be competent citizens, artists and scholars whether they were able to listen or not. I was one of those half-listeners, and this public note of gratitude is here because his teaching made this dictionary inevitable. See *Amer-Canadians*

BLUE JAYS

a) large, noisy but elegantly coloured scavengers found in suburbs and forests of Central Canada;

b) Toronto's baseball team and decade-long experiment in world class econopolitics. A Canadian brewery buys American and Latino millionaires to play baseball in a stadium where it's more fun to watch the top open and close than to follow what is, if we were sane, a children's game. The Jays win two World Series, but the millionaire ballplayers still leave town the moment the season's over. Then the brewery is sold to foreigners who care nothing for baseball or Toronto's world class aspirations, the millionaires go elsewhere to play, the team sinks to last place, and the fans quit coming to the stadium. Wasn't World Class great? No? Well, at least it got us the right to drink beer in public, which is about all World Class ever gets for anyone unless they're *very* wealthy.

BOARDS OF TRADE

Business cheerleaders and luncheon monkeys. Court of first resort for New Conservative supermen and anyone else wanting to propose the liquidation of the public sector.

BOLOGNA/BALONEY

What Ontario premier Michael Harris and a startling number of his admirers think poor people should not only consume but be grateful for.

LUCIEN BOUCHARD

Quebec Premier, former and still-functional leader of the federal Bloc Québécois and self-appointed Quebec Dauphin-in-Waiting. He's actually a small-town Quebec lawyer cut from same slinky cloth as Brian Mulroney, except that he has a French name, a more attractive wife and a wooden leg instead of a wooden personality. Bouchard's chief talent as a human being is a willingness to shove sharp pointed objects between the ribs of whomever stands between him and ascension to the throne of New France. He and his apparently estranged wife and children spend much of the year in the U.S., but then so do most wealthy Québécois. On the positive side, Bouchard doesn't appear to own any offshore-registered steamships.

BOWRON CLEARCUT

An officially-admitted 53 square kilometre but enormously larger clear-cut in Northern British Columbia that manages to be invisible to both the nearby towns and to those sleeping in the offices of the Provincial and Federal agencies responsible. The clearcut was, for a few years, with the Great Wall of China one of the two man-made objects visible from outer space with the naked eye. Many British Columbians want political union with the United States but a more likely fate is geographical and cultural union with the Bowron Clearcut.

BRAZILIAN BALLS

Toronto's wealthy socialites have recently taken to holding mini Mardi Gras charity balls at which guys who normally wear suits and stick knives between the ribs of the poor from behind dress up as women and openly fondle hired transvestites while their wives neck with swarthy dancers of both sexes and generally behave bizarrely. This is, one suspects, the Harris Tories' attempt to amalgamate high society and "a real fun time".

BRE-X

Yet another demonstration of the truths that
a)   it's impossible to cheat an honest person and
b)   that fools and their money are occasionally parted. . . .

BRITISH COLUMBIA

Canadian province permanently covered with water or heavy cloud to hide valleys and mountains denuded of trees by excessive logging. B.C. is lusted after by open space-craving Asian developers, water-starved California politicians, and by its own Native Indians, who want the right to exploit the remaining forests and fish like any other gang of financial hoodlums. Citizens and governments in B.C. are about equally prone to being bribed with their own resources by anyone who can propose a megaproject or real estate development big enough to convince them they'll be able to afford a long winter holiday in a warm, dry foreign country.

HONEST ED BROADBENT

Former federal NDP leader. He wasn't particularly honest and he wasn't much of leader in the 1988 federal election, when he traded Canadian sovereignty for NDP electoral hopes by refusing to participate in a coalition to defeat Mulroney's free trade initiative. The NDP has paid dearly—and deservedly—in subsequent elections.

KURT BROWNING

Browning was the most exciting and athletic figure skater Canada produced before Elvis Stojko came along. Because he was the first to display an on-ice sense of humour, a personality, and a temper without being forced into premature retirement, everyone assumes he's heterosexual. See *figure skaters*

BUNGLERS
See CSIS et al.

TED BYFIELD
Alberta culture hero. He's a presiding, if not exactly guiding spirit of right wing social and economic policy in Western Canada, and an all-round ass-kicking egomaniac. It's hard not to admire Byfield for saying what he means, not hiding who he wants to kick in the ass, and for doing a surprisingly good job of covering local culture in his Alberta and B.C. centred news magazines. Too bad his virtues aren't more common within the right wing in this country.

CABINET
The prime minister, his personal friends and some docile morons from the distant regions of the country. In recent years, this group has had the collective intelligence of a liquor cabinet, and the personality of a cardboard box.

CABLE
Coaxial-based nervous system of the global village, at least in urban areas. In the past ten years ownership in the Canadian cable industry has agglomerated, while Canadians have been offered a steadily growing variety of more or less identical choices in American programming. If anyone can find a redeeming property or quality anywhere in the cable television industry, I'd like to hear about it. Coaxial is soon to be replaced by fibreoptics, thus enlarging the fifty channel universe to five hundred channels without substantially enlarging anyone's range of programming choices.

CALGARY
Winner of Canadian Dallas lookalike contest, and home of Calgary Stampede, an annual event aimed at finding creative ways for drunk rednecks to kill and injure innocent horses.

JUNE CALLWOOD
Now-elderly white female journalist still young enough to tell people when to fuck off. Callwood insists on treating every issue with a combination of common sense and open-heartedness. This lifelong practice has recently bought her an excruciating load of undeserved trouble and abuse from Canada's cultural neotribalists and other self-impressed, bad-tempered social entrepreneurs. Vision Television confuses Callwood with Doris Day, and films her television show through cheesecloth and Vaseline.

ELSPETH CAMERON
Academic conference docent and author of sensationalized lives of several Canadian male literary figures. Cameron is not an important biographer nor a particularly complex character in her own loosely connected sheaf of semi-autobiographical short parodies of university life, but when she recently came out of the closet—or rather, burst from it with accompanying fireworks display and a total absence of discretion or second thoughts—she gave us a living demonstration, for the third or fourth time in her career, that Canada is among the very few countries in the world that has managed to become culturally misanthropic while remaining in every other respect as misogynist as Iraq and Kuwait. Wasn't the original goal of a university

education to teach people to precede action with thought, and to get rid of stupid, generalizing, ill-considered prejudices of *all* types?

DALTON CAMP

Red Tory journalist and bagman who was either the last person in Canada to swing from right to left, or the only one certain enough of his values to stand still in a political hurricane. Currently he's about the only political commentator in the country capable of surprising remarks. He's much reviled by the New Conservatives, who think common sense is a character flaw.

KIM CAMPBELL

B.C. Social Credit *wunderkind* and Canadian prime minister while Mila Mulroney was trying to find a fleet of trucks large enough to remove her furniture from 24 Sussex Drive. Campbell was slam-dunked in the 1993 general election because of the Mulroney legacy, but partly because her own people woke up to the fact that she was a Red Tory about to come out of the closet. Campbell went back to B.C., worked as a motivational speaker for various right-of-centre think tanks while she waited for an opening at one of the open-mouth radio stations. When that didn't exactly pan out, Chrétien gave her a job as director general in Los Angeles to get her out of the country for the Somalia Inquiry. She's the only Canadian politician of Cabinet rank to publicly discuss her loneliness and her sexual affairs as if she were mortal like the rest of us, but she's alas, not especially exciting in the nude.

BANK OF CANADA

Canadian branch plant of the IMF, World Bank, and U.S. Trade and Commerce department. Once a politically non-partisan agency charged with the mandate of balancing the need for employment and industrial growth with the banking and bond market sector desires for inflationary stability, it is now solely concerned with protecting (mostly offshore) investors against inflation while making life miserable for everyone else.

CANADA COUNCIL

Federal agency given the "arms-length" mandate, in the late 1950s, to nurture a distinct and authentic Canadian culture. Initially successful beyond its wildest dreams, the Canada Council is marked in the 1990s by diminishing budgets, a mysterious shortening in the length and strength of its arms, and an ongoing delusion that sixty percent of Canadians are French speaking.

CANADA POST

Formerly a public service designed to deliver letters, now a crown corporation dedicated to privatizing any delivery function that could break even or turn a profit. Currently a purveyor of junk mail, some badly-run courier services, and an international pioneer in neo-Visigoth corporate labour relations.

CANADA PRIME

The small zone boundaried by Kingston, Peterborough, London, Windsor and Niagara Falls inside which it is assumed that the maples are redder, the brick buildings larger, incomes higher and CBC signals stronger than elsewhere in the country.

CANADIAN CENTRE
FOR POLICY ALTERNATIVES

NDP-sympathetic think tank housed in five or six cardboard boxes somewhere in the Ottawa area. Consists mostly of trade union research directors and out-of-fashion university professors. Usually six months late on issues due to lack of funding and worker safety-related concerns.

THE CANADIAN ENCYCLOPEDIA

A Toronto-centric view of Canada as recognized by those Canadians who own Volvo station wagons. It was first published in the late 1980s by Mel Hurtig and is now, despite its considerable merit, perpetually to be found on remainder tables in discount bookstores. Now available on CD-ROM, if you're impressed by technological advances of that sort.

THE CANADIAN IDENTITY

Sorry, but there isn't a grand metaphor that can adequately describe the character of Canada or its people. We aren't unified, we're not monocultural, chromal or cytal, and we're not supposed to be. We're simply people who live north of the Great Lakes or the 49th parallel. We don't wear sandals after September 15th unless we're on drugs or outside the country, we're not Survivors, Bush-Gardeners, tiles in an Ottawa mosaic or base metals in an American melting pot. But somewhere, deep in our collective and individual souls, we are a people who understand that when you mix big metaphors with politics, you get bullshit, and you get dead people.

CANCON

Regulations imposed on the Canadian radio and television industries to ensure a minimum of Canadian-produced content on Canadian communications systems. After a slow start and a decade of forcing innocent people to listen to Anne Murray on the radio and watch her on what seemed like biweekly television specials, the technology base and industrial economies-of-scale emerged to permit Canadian music to be as slick and well-produced as any in the world. The CRTC will probably be deregulated out of existence before the same thing can happen in television—and before the general population realizes that some forms of cultural regulation can be wildly—and profitably—successful.

CANFILM

Canadian filmmakers make interesting films that actually are distinctly, or rather, uniquely, Canadian without being precious or coy. They're also often surprisingly kinky, e.g., Atom Egoyan's *Exotica*, John Greyson's *Lilies*, Robert LePage's *Le Confessional*, Denis Arcand's *Jesus of Montreal*, and Lynne Stopkewich's *Kissed*, along with the now large and definitely strange opus of David Cronenberg. The problem is that with the exception of Cronenberg, the films aren't distributed, in Canada or anywhere else. See *Jack Valenti*

CANLIT

A phenomenon that suffers from a set of attributes and conditions largely the opposite to those of CanFilm: timid convolutions along a narrow conduit of preciousness studded with too self-conscious symbols and themes the products of which are then, alas, *over*-distributed. CanLit began as part of an enlightened program begun in the late 1950s by federalists who realized that Canada's best method of defending its boundaries would be to secure its cultural identity. One of the logical ways of doing this was to begin to nurture its artistic community within the nation's borders rather than exporting talent to the U.S. and Britain or exterminating it. As federal programs go, this one was wildly successful and cost-effective even if it has probably less often nurtured artists than it has encouraged a lot of idiots to be idiotic on acid-free paper.

Somewhere in the 1970s, a critical mass emerged within the Canadian writing community, and Canada began to produce a small number of brilliant writers, a moderate number of good writers, and a huge horde of college professors who wrote poems and short stories about one another which they then began to teach to incoming generations of students who grow up to believe that literature is silly and irrelevant. This timid enterprise, not to be confused with "writing going on in Canada" alas, is what CanLit has devolved to. Oh well. Still cheaper than the F-18, which enlightens no one and defends nothing except the apparent right of macho war-dorks to burn up a lot of aviation fuel.

CAPE BRETON

Former Nova Scotia fishing and coal-mining disaster zone, more recently a sinkhole for government pork barrel remainders and half-assed UIC schemes that merely piss off the locals even more. Inhabited by lobsters and permanently vacationing unemployed Newfoundlanders and other victims of cod fishery collapse.

CASCADIA

B.C. separatist name for post-Canada Republic of British Columbia, Washington State, Oregon and Northern California. If Cascadia ever comes into existence, it will designate most of B.C. for water storage. Happily, no one in the U.S. Northwest believes B.C. would be stupid enough to join.

CBC

Canadian Broadcasting Corporation: A small group of beleaguered, bearded males and expensively dressed females from the upper middle classes who operate a vestigial communications network from a series of glamorous half-empty buildings in Toronto, Montreal, Vancouver and a diminishing number of other Canadian centres. The corporation is now under permanent siege from the federal government and private sector media, aided by CBC senior management, whose chief role is to pretend that the network remains viable, fire any staff who don't spend at least two days a week in the Toronto building and send around memos counseling broadcast staff to lick the boots of government officials no matter what they do or say.

CBC DIVAS

A nearly extinct subspecies of usually blonde, voluptuous middle-aged women able to sing in tune 85 percent of the time: Juliette, Lorraine Thompson, Marg Osburne, the Allen Sisters. Their disappearance is an indirect result of CRTC CanCon regulations and the subsequent maturation of an authentic Canadian music industry.

CBC MANAGEMENT

At one time CBC was run without any visible management. Since Marcel Masse set in motion the machinery to exterminate the CBC, the corporation has been run by a series of political bumboys and ill-trained management surgeons. First went the extremities that once put the CBC in touch with the communities it should serve, then they overbuilt the physical plants in Montreal, Vancouver and Toronto. The CBC is the best argument going that management does more harm than good.

ROCH CARRIER

Once upon a time, this man wrote a wonderful story about a hockey sweater. Then he studied management, got into managing military colleges, and finally became the executive director of the Canada Council. This is a sad story getting sadder.

JEAN CHAREST

Former eager beaver junior Cabinet minister in the Brian Mulroney government, and sole brand-name survivor of 1993 electoral wipe-out of the Progressive Conservative Party. Now Conservative leader, his 1997 pre-election makeover left him slimmer, nastier and supposedly believing that rescinding gun control legislation would make him as popular as Preston Manning. The 1997 election results left him to run the Eastern Canada wing of the Reform Party, which, given that he loathes Preston Manning, is about what he deserves. Still looks like a too-eager junior Cabinet minister.

CHARLOTTETOWN ACCORD

Brian Mulroney's follow-up foul-up after the Meech Lake Accord died. The Accord has been called the only recorded instance of an elected government trying to overthrow the country that elected it. Luckily, enough people caught on during the referendum with which Mulroney tried to gain national acceptance for this demolition permit that the referendum went down to defeat and the Accord expired like its predecessor. Among those who didn't catch on were the Ottawa-based mass media and most of the other junior governments across the country, the former deluded by too many cocktail parties and the latter by their eagerness to obtain additional powers. Mulroney must have had one hell of a drug supplier working his side of the table to get the premiers to agree to go in front of the public and get shot up over that nation-breaking deal. There was, to be fair, not all that much to distrust in the terms of the Charlottetown Accord, but a great deal to distrust in the clowns who created and hawked it.

CHARTERS

At the heart of the 1982 constitutional repatriation was Pierre Trudeau's Federalist wish to formalize democratic processes and institutions in the face of an uncertain future, and to place them in the hands of a strong central government. The two major elements of that were an agreement that would bind Quebec to Confederation, and to enshrine a Charter of Rights and Freedoms with specifics similar to those in the United States as the core of Canada's legal and constitutional structure.

The repatriation process foundered when Quebec recognized that the Charter would impinge on elements of the province's civil laws. Moreover, Quebec could not agree to those provisions of the constitution that governed future constitutional alterations, and the series of subsequent conciliatory maneuvers meant to bring the province in and to pacify its separatists has been used by an ascendant conservative movement to weaken the central government by devolving its powers to the provinces.

The Charter of Rights and Freedoms itself has been used by the professional classes to ensure that existing and incoming lawyers will remain fully employed until the 22nd Century. It also guarantees the right of everyone to be offended by any and everything, and to litigate their grievances. Quebec, meanwhile, which has operated under the Napoleonic Code in matters of civil law since 1763, has continued to be uncooperative about the Charter, possibly because it would infringe on the long-cherished wish of certain Québécois males to return Cardinal Richelieu and Louis XIV to power.

CHARTER OF RIGHTS AND FREEDOMS

From one point of view, an attempt to replace British common law with an approximation of American statutory guarantees. There's a danger that the Charter will merely guarantee every Canadian a plague of lawyers, along with the right to compulsory litigation. But a less cynical view is to acknowledge that it is useful for a group of people planning to live together to formalize the ground rules, and to declare (and make actionable) that they're permitted to say and write whatever they want even if some people are offended.

Yet even an actionable Charter is limited by the culture in which it operates—in Canada's case, an aggressive business culture that is part of a global economic revolution that characteristically tries to undermine nation-states wherever and whenever the nation-states impinge on the unfettered activities of the market. Even though it's largely a moveable abstraction often colliding with an irresistible market economy, the Charter nonetheless helps to sustain a way of talking about life that we abandon at our peril, and it provides individuals and groups in civil society some protection against arbitrary, addled, and/or whimsical legislators.

ECONOMIC CHARTER
The 1991 attempt by Brian Mulroney to
a) enshrine principle of no taxation for the corporate sector;
b) ensure that the right to excessive real estate and corporate profits supercede all other rights and
c) ship more of Ottawa's rotten federal bananas to naively eager-for-power provincial governments.

FRENCH LANGUAGE CHARTER
Draconian set of regulations passed by the Quebec legislature aimed at protecting the French Language from those English peegs—and from civility, common sense and fully-awake people like Mordecai Richler.

DON CHERRY
Canadian hockey's one-man Beavis and Butthead. A man who can perch at the edge of self-destruction on national television as long as Cherry has isn't stupid. Whatever else Cherry is—and he's many things, most of them direct and decent—he's life's

revenge on people like Perrin Beatty and other puffed egos and stuffed shirts around the country. He may crash and burn now that he's a widower.

JEAN CHRETIEN

Trudeau-era federal Cabinet minister often trotted out to prove Trudeau didn't really have anything against the common people. From there, Chrétien evolved from being yesterday's man through the Mulroney era to become closet-Conservative Party Prime Minister in 1993. Apparently a nice man who phones Queen Elizabeth for comfort when he's upset, he's been difficult to distinguish from Mulroney save for his joual bark that somehow convinces Canadians he's sincere, and that sincerity is worth the powder required to blow it to hell. He's good at working small crowds, better at working over small people in crowds, but he sends out his wife to foil would-be assassins. Otherwise, he has demonstrated few tangible qualities of leadership not evident in members of the weasel family.

CHRISTMAS

Formerly the birth date of Jesus Christ, now reduced to the retail sector's respite from bankruptcy. So many Christmas carols have now been banned because they offend Canada's minorities that our children are growing up believing that this holiday is about a fat dwarf who lives at the north pole during the summer and works the malls through November and December. Christmas is followed by Boxing Day, which too many of us believe is the one day in the year when we can beat up on family members and not be jailed for it.

CIGARETTES

The only role a clear majority of Canadians—or is it merely Canadian bureaucrats and health professionals—now want their governments to have is to make smoking cigarettes a semi-criminal activity. The relative price of cigarettes from province to province is determined by the Calvinism of presiding governments, and by the number of border-straddling Native Indian reserves.

THE CIURLUINI SISTERS

Jennifer and Cynthia Dale, locally over-exposed Canadian television actresses who can't seem to get steady work in the U.S. Hard to find a Canadian male over thirty and under seventy-five who doesn't think they're babes.

CIVIC POLITICS

Oedipal zone of Canadian politics in which the only rule is that a civic government's political ideology must be 180 degrees from that of the Provincial government in power. Civic government has few real powers and rewards, huge responsibilities, and anybody with the political talent of a chimpanzee is instantly scooped up by senior governments.

GLEN CLARK

B.C. premier after Michael Harcourt fell on the party sword to cover up the NDP's corrupt fundraising practices. Clark quickly moved the public apparatus of his office from Victoria to a locale close to the stock exchange in downtown Vancouver and began to hold regular news conferences designed to manipulate the B.C. media. He may seem in most respects as right wing as Preston Manning, but his true problem is that he's incompetent at both right and left wing behaviours. That B.C.'s media have been attempting to exterminate him since he took office for being slick and NDP at the same time shouldn't dilute his importance as the operator of the only political constituency in the country that hasn't officially bellied up the globalist bar and declared the triumph of kick-the-poor capitalism.

JOE CLARK

Short-term Conservative Prime Minister, aged boy wonder and Federal Minister of Suicidal Initiatives for Brian Mulroney during the "Dismantle Canada" program. Reputedly the wittiest and nicest man in Mulroney's government, which, given the competition, wasn't much of an accomplishment. Married Maureen McTeer, which didn't turn out to be the sort of accomplishment it promised to be.

ADRIENNE CLARKSON

CBC doyenne and public sector impresario. If you can forget how long she's been representing the ruling classes in Canadian arts, you'll notice how consistently she's tried to embrace what's radical and wild in our culture rather than tiptoeing away from it like everyone else of her age and background.

CN TOWER

Was this monstrosity built because Ontario rests on a gradual southerly slope and building a tower was the only way to transmit radio, television and other data signals? Or was there an egomaniac with a big-penis complex who had too much access to competent engineers and public funds? There is no other public structure in the world so public as the CN Tower, nor so badly explained and understood.

BRUCE COCKBURN

Anglican bishop of Canadian music.

TOM COCHRANE

Peter Mansbridge had Cochrane's *Life Is a Highway* played in his dressing room before reading the news while he was breaking up with Wendy Mesley and planning to push then-cohost Pamela Wallin off the plank. Wonder what that says about Tom Cochrane—other than that people over forty really can't be trusted with rock 'n' roll.

COD FISHERY

Defunct east-coast ecosystem destroyed by lack of stock conservation, weakness in controlling European fishing fleets in Canadian waters, badly off-base fisheries department cod and halibut counts, and all those fisherman lying about what they've got in the bottom of their boats.

LEONARD COHEN

Neurotic Montreal Christian/Buddhist poet, novelist, folksinger, and rock star who has been able, through sheer originality, to be any and all of those things sucessfully on a lasting basis. There are about seven women in Canada under fifty who wouldn't sleep with him.

DOUG COLLINS

Eminence grise aggrieved white guy and former west-coast labour reporter who fell off his bar stool one night and woke up somewhere to the right of Benito Mussolini. This is a guy that Allan Fotheringham is ashamed to call an ex-friend.

COMEDIANS

Canada, not so surprisingly, produces a disproportionate per-capita number of good comedians (at a rate about equivalent to the ratio of Stasi agents to citizens of the former East Germany). *Kids in the Hall*, sctv, *Saturday Night Live, Codco, Royal Canadian Air Farce* and *This Hour Has 22 Minutes* have too good an uncanned laugh-track record over the years to be merely an accident. As in any situation of a beaver and an elephant cohabiting a continent, the beaver has to be pretty funny to survive. Naturally, the Canadian comic genius rests with social satire, and likewise naturally, comedy's geographic centre is Newfoundland. Eventually, all the Canadian comics go to America to seek their fortune, and eventually become much less funny. Conventional stand-up comics of Canadian origin, meanwhile, are no funnier than any other kind.

COMMUNISM

Before 1989, Communism was the threat that kept Canada in NATO, and our technologically superfluous armed forces in business. Since 1989, it has been redemonized by the new conservatives to mean that tiny part of the human spirit that wants to treat the poor decently, take care of the elderly and infirm, and other behaviours that conflict with the dictatorship of the entrepreneurs.

COMMUNITY REINVESTMENT

In the U.S., banks are obliged by American law to reinvest some of their profits within the communities from which they were harvested. Sounds reasonable enough, but the Canadian Banker's Association seems to think that applying this same logic to Canada's chartered banks is 2/3rds of a Communist takeover all in itself. Hmmm. *Can* banx change? That's the wrong question. The right questions are, *What would possibly make banks change while they're being guaranteed astronomical profits?* And *Why would they agree to changes?*

CONFERENCE BOARD OF CANADA

No one should be fooled by the opaque name. These guys don't organize conferences. They're a thinktank run by and for Canada's chartered banks, and it represents bank interests as if they were a theological tenet identical to public well-being.

STOMPIN' TOM CONNORS

He wrote *The Hockey Song*, and he writes exclusively about Canada. But he looks like William Burroughs, sings about as well, and no one from west of Winnipeg knows who he is. But the country would be poorer without him, particularly if someone could figure out a way to cross him with Bruce Cockburn.

CONSERVATIVES

Theoretically, conservatives are those people who believe that things should stay where they are and how they are. It therefore requires a subtle mind to distinguish conservatives from social democrats in Canada, who believe things shouldn't ever change,

budgets shouldn't be cut or programs massacred and/or cancelled. The difference, aside from cosmetic matters of car preference (social democrats prefer Swedish cars, while Conservatives
prefer German or Japanese cars, or Oldsmobiles) is that conservatives are those who believe that wealth should stay in the hands
of those who have it now. See *New Conservatives*, *NeoCons*, *Red
Tories*, and *Conservative Intellectuals*

PROGRESSIVE CONSERVATIVES

Oxymoronic political movement based on the theory that life is
best viewed with one nostril up the ass of the current U.S. president and the other up the posterior of the nearest tax accoun-
tant. Nearly exterminated in the 1993 election, still on life
support (or rather, corporate support) after the election in 1997.

CONSTITUTIONAL INITIATIVES

A process of national dissolution begun in the late 1970s by Pierre
Trudeau, who imagined that repatriating the British North America Act from the utterly indifferent British would somehow make
Canada stronger and more virile. Trudeau's other intention—
which was to make an accommodation with French-speaking
Canada that would narrow the civil separation between English-
speaking Canada created in 1763 when Britain permitted Quebec
to continue civil administration through the Napoleonic Code—
may have been honourable in his logical, Jesuit fashion. Today it
merely provides an object lesson in what paves the road to hell.
In the late 1980s, the Mulroney government mounted a series of
right wing constitutional initiatives—the Meech Lake deal and
the Charlottetown Accord—designed to disperse powers to the

provinces and make the taxation of the corporate sector impossible. Destructive as these were in themselves, the public debate over them served as a smokescreen to the signing of "trade" agreements with the United States and other countries that have made reaching a constitutional agreement with Quebec superfluous. By putting all our important national institutions under the control of multinational corporations and their policy apparati, we've created a central government unable to tax anyone but its individual citizens, and one that is frankly reluctant to govern the country. On the other hand, individual Canadians did get a Charter of Rights and Freedoms. And the way things are going, it may be a good idea to have a set of civil guarantees on the books that are actionable rather than merely petitionable. See *bananas, Charlottetown Accord, Meech Lake*

CONSTITUTIONAL ASYMMETRY

Jean Chrétien's new code for "Distinct Society". I mean, really, guys, haven't Canadians already demonstrated that they're tired of constitutional mumbo-jumbo? And anyway, you build cultural inequality in a constitution. Or let me revise that slightly. You can, for a while. But a constitution that has it won't work for much longer than the 1973 Yugoslav constitution did. This is not to be confused with the issue of *democratic* asymmetry, which can be a civilized response to physical conditions, e.g., paying workers with children more than workers without children, giving mothers maternity leave, etc. Instead of trying to hoodwink everyone, why not remove the posturing, rhetoric, megalomania, insanity, resentment, ill-will on all sides, and rely on the one resource nobody has yet tried to use: common sense.

CONVERGENCE

A cultural *faux*-phenomenon that is designed to applaud communications technologies that colonize one another's functions, so that, for instance, your coffee-maker can wake you up in the morning with elevator music, and not incidentally, convince you that life is better and more exciting. The introduction of microchips into mechanical technologies has had some minor benefits, but if you listen to the corporate futurists, it's going to solve every problem from fridge stink to international hunger. In fact, it's going to make the basic devices we need for survival more complex, more expensive and less reliable. It will also lead to complicated litigation with the CRTC and the FCC and result in more corporate raiding and goldfish-eating riots within the telecommunications industry. Is it really worth all this trouble just so we can have simulated sex with our toasters?

PETER COOK

Globe & Mail three-monkey apologist for indefensibly high profits, astronomical corporate salaries, various trade agreements, and anything American, provided it isn't black, poor or refuses to read business books.

SHEILA COPPS

Bilingual MP from a powerful Hamilton, Ontario family, Federal Heritage minister and recently drop-kicked former deputy P.M. Copps has been the recipient of more tasteless parliamentary and Ottawa press club insults and innuendoes than any woman this side of Margaret Trudeau. She is also an apprehended and self-confessed liar, which makes her more or less unique in Ottawa political circles. If Copps is even remotely successful at protecting Canadian culture, she'll likely become prime minister early in the 21st century. But she'll have to govern from a small office provided by Moody's Bond Rating Service, because that'll be all that's left of the federal government when Chrétien and Paul Martin, Jr. get finished with it.

CO-PRODUCTION

Canadian produced television in which Canadian urban landscapes are Americanized, then populated with American stars, Canadian bit actors, vampires, alien invaders, homicidal mutants and various American peace officers.

TERRANCE CORCORAN

Globe & Mail Tweedle-Dumb business columnist. Most rightwing mouthpiece columnist in Canada. He's also the only serious Libertarian who appears regularly in any North American newspaper.

MICHAEL COREN

Charter aggrieved white guy Coren started off public life as a British fop, writing a biography of British conservative Catholic jingoist G.K. Chesterton, becoming a Toronto media presence by dressing up—and shooting off his mouth—as if it were the 1890s. He's currently attracting litigation as an open mouth radio host, newspaper columnist and all-round intellectual soccer thug. If just one person in the Toronto cultural community had bothered to read or reread Chesterton a few years ago, Coren would have been laughed out of the country. He's quick to resort to hysterical ideology—the typical result of sincerity mixed with a lack of talent—and has become a kind of miniature rottweiler for the much more powerful but shadowy figures who find it convenient to have him in the public eye.

CORPORATE COMEDIANS

No, not the federal Cabinet. Canadian corporations are pioneering the practice of hiring comedians as motivational speakers to tell inspirational corporate jokes at meetings and seminars. Normal people would think they've stumbled into another business prayer meeting, but there you are. The fad actually started with former Monty Python comic John Cleese deciding to make business instructional videos during a bout of suicidal depression.

COTTAGES

Residents of Ontario and Quebec can't be certified as fully middle class unless they spend their summer weekends clogging the highways to get to recreational properties that must be situated no less than two hours from their primary residences. Maritimers are generally too poor and sensible to own recreational property, the prairie provinces don't have recreational areas worth owning property in, while B.C. residents either haven't been settled long enough to find anywhere to build on, or believe that recreational property means buying highway-clogging Windbags, harbour-polluting sailboats or neck-breaking trail bikes or Skidoos. Where cottages exist in B.C., they're called cabins, and they don't have running water. The exception is the Whistler ski area, where they're called chalets and necessitate membership in an extremist right wing political party.

DOUG COUPLAND

Vancouver writer who coined the phrase that identified the demographic group now in the mid-30s and thus about to, in Dante's phrase, throw away their crutches and stop being so passive. The first twenty pages of Coupland's book *Generation X* are among the most accurate and efficient pages of cultural history ever written, and Coupland has the best eye for cultural details of his or any other generation of Canadian writers.

ANDREW COYNE

Junior Doberman-at-large who left the *Globe & Mail* to chew on leftist bones for Conrad Black's various newspapers. He's fond of peering down his long aristocratic snout at those not so hip as he to the new Darwinist realities of post-Canada Canada. Coyne is what David Frum would be if Frum's parents had gone ahead with the growth hormone therapy. He's perhaps the only male conservative intellectual in the country who isn't at least twenty pounds overweight.

TOLLER CRANSTON

Three little old ladies in Northern Manitoba haven't figured out that Cranston is gay, and that's only because the bookmobile doesn't stock his autobiography. He was, in his day, the world's best and most innovative male skater, but his obvious if not exactly open orientation led to a forced retirement. Too bad it's only now the world is ready for Toller — as a skater, not as an interior decorator.

CREATING JOBS

What governments pretend they're doing while slashing threads in the social net and sucking up to the banking community. If asked where the jobs are, politicians and their flacks solemnly point to the small business sector they're helping the banks deprive of oxygen and claim that creating jobs is *their* responsibility.

CRTC

(Canadian Radio-TeleCommunications Commission) Supposedly it exists to protect Canadians from the total commercialization of telecommunications. In reality the CRTC has been in so passionate an embrace with the cable companies for the last decade that a KY pipeline to the hearing rooms is being planned.

CSIS

See bunglers (also Bozos, idiots, paranoids, etc.).

CTV

Originally and until recently a quarrelsome agglomeration of private television stations huddled around Harvey Kirck, Lloyd Robertson and other news-reading blocks of wood, while relying on American drama and game shows for revenue. Currently a battleground for communications giants, along with a showpiece scrap for control between the Eaton/Bassett families and a B.C.-based corporation of more shadowy ownership, all of whom continue to agree only that Canadian television ought to resemble American television wherever possible, and that Canadian production, where necessary, should be coproduced schlock in which Toronto and Vancouver are made to resemble Cleveland, Seattle and other north-of-California cities.

THE CUBAN MISSILE CRISIS

The point in history (October 1962) when the U.S. reintroduced the Monroe Doctrine, and Canadians lost their independent foreign policy and began to crouch under tables and desks like good Americans during civil defence exercises.

A BRIEF SERMON ON CULTURE

Culture operates in many ways and at different levels of public, political and private consciousness. In a strict sense, it is the sum total of what we do, which, because we're doing it, makes the idea meaningless. Toilet seats, for instance, are cultural artifacts, and whether men lift them when they urinate or leave them down and sprinkle them to annoy women is a serious cultural behaviour.

A more practical definition is to see culture as the collection of deliberate behaviours and cognitive instruments that dissuade us from bludgeoning one another when we don't agree on matters of fact and opinion. In this sense culture regulates our politics, our commerce and our sociality, and where effective, separates and gentles their differing ambitions and compelling moral and technical codes. Active culture is when we think about what we do and why we do it—a condition altogether too rare these days.

Many people today associate culture with the fine arts, which is an understandable but pernicious error. Art and culture are not one and the same, as anyone who has sat in the audience at the symphony or slept through a poetry reading will recognize. Neither the orchestra players, the poets, nor the audience are terribly interested in how to keep us from ripping out one another's jugulars. On the other hand, you never quite know what that viola player is thinking about, or if that aging matron in the sequined dress might be imagining a better world and not merely pondering the wisdom of joining the blue rinse brigade. I've seen significant acts of culture while shopping in a supermarket. That man over there, frowning over the lack of unbleached coffee filters, for instance.

CULTURE (AMERICAN)

Educated Canadians adore American culture unless and until they are caught with it in their homes and/or brains. The rest of Canada just sucks in American entertainment with the air supply and enjoys the usually superior technical values.

CULTURE (BEER)

Most likely replacement for Canada's indigenous culture, if the multinationals get their way: go to the beach, park the Camaro, crank up the ghettoblaster, open the icebox, crack open a beer and party on. That this makes Kool & the Gang a major culture hero, or that you spend the other 350 days a year working two McJobs to make your car payments doesn't seem to be an issue. This is something subtly different than business culture, which involves 24 hour-a-day obsessing over one's investments with a cellphone jammed in one's ear.

CULTURE (MURKAN)

Murkans have a longstanding desire to exterminate Canada's indigenous behaviours, as we saw most recently during the FTA and NAFTA negotiations. Murkan cultural proponents recognize that the chief and most lethal export of the United States is its culture, a fact that seems to have eluded Canadian political leaders after Pierre Trudeau. Leading cultural Murkans: Michael Eisner, Jack Valenti, Carla Hills. Canadian arranger/musical producer David Foster is an honorary Murkan. See *Murkans*

CULTURE (GLOBAL)

If the economic globalization that seems to be replacing the nation-state we call Canada were also introducing cosmopolitan notions about culture and community, there would be little resistance to it. But that is not what is happening. There is no global culture, but rather the supplanting of civil community, culture and cosmopolitanism with economic competition as a moral system, tribalisms in a variety of dependent pathologies as our means of socialization, and the treatment of all life's other complexities with the tools of chartered accountancy. It won't work.

CULTURAL EXEMPTIONS

Under intense pressure from the solid majority of Canadians who wanted local alternatives to the culture of Donald Duck and Roseanne, the Mulroney government negotiated a clause that exempted cultural institutions and industries from the terms of both the Canada/U.S. FTA and NAFTA. Or so it seemed. The exemption effectively froze funding at 1988 levels, and prevented Canada from mounting new protection mechanisms. As the other machinery of government was dismantled, leaving the federal government unable to generate revenue, culture budgets have been cut, while many of the protective mechanisms in place before the "exemption" was created have rapidly rusted into irrelevance.

CULTURAL POLICY (pre-Mulroney)

Until the late 1950s, Canada had no self-conscious culture except at the CBC and within a few wealthy enclaves in Montreal and Toronto. From that point through 1984, culture was gradually recognized as a cheap and effective form of national defence. The result was that the Canada Council and other funding agencies were given 1/5th the funding required to be effective; Pierre Trudeau created FIRA to screen foreign ownership of Canada's cultural and industrial essentials, and a series of piecemeal measures were created to prevent takeovers of cultural industries. FIRA became the ostensible focus of the FTA's successful dismantling of national sovereignty during the late 1980s, while cultural subsidies were ceilinged and then forced into fiscal free-fall by 1990s budget cuts. Most of the other instruments have either been sidestepped or declared illegal by GATT and other trade bodies.

CULTURAL POLICY (post Mulroney)

Profitable tourist-pleasing activities that convince wealthy residents they live in a world class city, or permit them not to think about either the present or future consequences of their lifestyle.

Best exemplified by people with violins, or out-of-town movie stars who can sing in tune, attend cocktail parties and have large breasts. Bistro 990, Massey Hall and Princess of Wales Theatre in Toronto, plus the Ford Centres in Vancouver and suburban Toronto are the imaginative epicentres of pre-millennium arts culture.

CURRENT ACCOUNT BALANCE (CAB)

Whether it's a whole country or just you and me, CAB is the amount of money going out subtracted from the amount of money coming in. When it comes to national economies, the CAB is the truest indicator of commercial well-being if viewed over a reasonable length of time. It's also the least-reported economic statistic in Canada. While StatsCan is willing to tell us that we have a trade surplus, and the corporations use it to convince us that the economy is performing well even though we have a huge deficit and crippling unemployment, we never hear a word about the woeful condition of our national CAB. If we did, we'd figure out that the outflow of profits to offshore corporations has been impoverishing the country for the last fifteen years, and has made us incapable of paying our debts. Try to extract the numbers on *this* out of StatsCan.

TOM D'AQUINO

Executive Director of Small Business Alliance of Canada regularly trotted out at news conferences and business conventions by the corporate media to prove that Canadian small businesses are against everything that is logically in their interest if it is tainted by NDP endorsement or other communist plots.

ROBERTSON DAVIES

Faux-British Canadian novelist, recently deceased. Why was it that a man born and raised in Canada who spent less than four years at Oxford spoke like a Bloomsbury fop a half-century later? And how was it that no one ever teased him for it? Davies led an unreasonably fortunate life, one that had so debilitating an effect on his common sense that late in life he conflated sneezes and orgasms, and died believing that one can see the world adequately from the hallways of the English Department.

DEGRASSI STREET

Street in Toronto's east end used for the location of an initially accurate series of CBC television dramas about the urban young and not-wealthy. Unfortunately the actors grew up and turned into smaller replicas of Al Waxman, and the series ended up looking like Melrose Place with a very lite film of grit. Degrassi OAP is reportedly in the works.

DESMARAIS; PAUL, ANDRE

Chair and deputy chair of Power Corporation. If you can figure out what these guys are about, let the NDP brain trust know right away, eh?

JOHN DIEFENBAKER

Conservative Canadian prime minister 1957-63 who dismantled Canadian government R&D capacity and transformed previously independent Canadian foreign policy to the mewling, puking synchophancy to U.S. foreign policy we know today. He is buried in recently vacated Saskatchewan to reduce the danger of his grave being desecrated by Canadians who recognize what his cowardice and egomania brought down on us.

ROSIE DIMANNO

Toronto Star columnist and reporter at large, and the best conventional journalist in the country. Her gig at the *Toronto Star* apparently allows her to write on any subject that interests her. In a better world she'd be a cultural treasure: she gets the facts and doesn't fall for the factoids, uncovers the hidden stories, and writes so well you don't see the energy of her language. She's the only newspaper writer in the country who doesn't want to be a television star, and she dresses, er, more tastefully than Pierre Berton.

CELINE DION

The Carmen Miranda of Quebec music, and a role model for musical anorexics and others prone to depression and compulsive typing. No relation to either Whitney Houston or Edith Piaf, Dion may represent Quebec's cultural future after it leaves Canada. See *David Foster*

DISTINCT SOCIETIES

Semantic maneuver by the Federal government designed to legitimize Quebec separatist need to suppress foreign languages, build hydroelectric megaprojects, and be exploited by France and the United States rather than Canada. Every other political entity in Canada, including the Boy Scouts, has subsequently demanded the same right. In fact, our constitution, our education system and our mothers have been guaranteeing this for fifty years. Wouldn't it be more constructive if we were asking to

be "unusual", "attractive", "reasonable" or—dare we ask this?—
"functional" societies? So here's the solution: Quebec is a *francophone* society.

DIVISIBILITY

A popular practice in the former Yugoslavia, it has recently been
introduced into Canadian politics over Quebec. Lucien Bouchard
announces that Canada is divisible, Chrétien retaliates by saying that Quebec is divisable, too—and so on down into the sew-
ers of opportunism with Preston Manning and Jacques Parizeau.
Divisibility means denying one's metaphorical ox can possibly
be gored while jamming its horn deep into the adjacent ox. In
the real world, fools can divide anything.

DNA EVIDENCE

Relatively new scientific method of determining who the real
criminal isn't, mostly, as with Guy Paul Morin, who was wrongly
convicted of murdering Christine Jessop a decade ago. DNA evidence is also, apparently, quite reliable in determining that some
criminals are convicted simply because the authorities don't like
their intransigence in the face of threats and accusations.

THE DOLLAR

About 75 cents when things are going really well. The goal of
NAFTA is to make the Canadian dollar indistinguishable from
the Mexican peso.

DOMED STADIUMS

Smarting under allegations that it is colder in Canada than in the U.S. and that Canadian cities would not be able to get and keep major sports franchises without an indoor stadium, planning geniuses across the country have built three domed stadiums. The scorecard so far? Lost franchises: 4 (3 soccer, 1 football). Threatened: 3 (2 football, 1 baseball). Gained: none. On the positive side, it gives Canadians at least three locations where they can attend monster tractor pulls in the middle of winter, and the domes provide suitably unhealthy but year-round environments for outdoor evangelical revivals, religious conventions, and airborne fungi of a wide and toxic variety.

A CANADIAN DOOMSDAY SCENARIO

Fourteen or fifteen codependent province-like banana republics, each clamouring for more dignity, independence and money from a shrinking and barely operational central government while untaxed foreign multinationals extract the profits and resources from the hinterlands and shovel the remnant industrial base out of Southern Ontario to Mexico and the U.S. A succession of increasingly befuddled and incompetent Prime Ministers treat the separatists in Quebec as paranoic demigods who must be kept within the union even if it means feeding them a steady diet of cake. Meanwhile, British Columbians rumble about joining Cascadia, Alberta shifts its loyalties and its civilities toward The Montana Militia and Standard Oil, and other regions of the country whine about leaving Confederation even though no one else would possibly want them. Geez, we're halfway there. . . .

GARTH DRABINSKY

Cultural hype-meister and self-promoter, about whom this book officially has no critical opinion except that Andrew Lloyd Weber should be banned from Canadian theatres as the defoliant he is. Drabinsky is affectionately known as Garth Vader in the Canadian theatre community. Other nicknames tend to be less affectionate.

GILLES DUCEPPE

Foot-in-mouth successor to Lucien Bouchard as Bloc Québécois leader. Cites Mexico as an illustration of how business can continue despite "trouble", and will probably be the first in line to offer Carlos Salinas political asylum when and if the other shoe drops. Let's hope Duceppe *never* gets into serious "trouble" himself. . . .

DUE SOUTH

Co-production aberration in which a Canadian and American actor actually make Canada and Canadians seem kinder, more decent, more intelligent and better looking than America and Americans. Stranger still, the show is well-written, and the setting is the United States. This is about as good as television coproduction gets, folks, and the alacrity and frequency with which Due South gets cancelled and then renewed bears a credible resemblance to the Chinese fire drill.

MIKE DUFFY

Aggrieved white guy, gourmet newsperson and political contortionist. Despite being at least 5000 donuts over the legal limit,

Duffy has been able to fit comfortably in the breast pockets of two successive prime ministers and anyone else willing to slash a budget or enhance corporate powers. Duffy believes that the media is a left-wing conspiracy, which may indicate that it's time to ship him out of Ottawa for a reality check even if it requires a special rail car.

MARIO DUMONT

Youth leader during the 1995 Quebec referendum. What are the most important questions to ask people like Dumont? How about *Have you ever had a homosexual experience? And if not, why not?*

ALAN EAGLESON

Hockey, er, legend. That the Canadian and/or U.S. legal systems have taken this long to have criminal charges laid against this manipulator of dull young men's investments and crippled old men's pensions is incomprehensible. Or is this yet another piece of circumstantial evidence that the firebugs are in control of the fire hall?

EASTER

They used to let the kids out of school, and Christians went around feeling gloomy—first because Christ was dead, and second because the Church was trying to convince everybody that he'd come back once, and was going to do it again so he could kill everyone who didn't co-operate with the Church. Now Easter has something to do with egg-laying bunnies and support

for the sugar confection industry. Not clear whether this is a cultural advance or setback.

EATON BOYS
Rich boys who, after bringing the family department store chain
to the brink of bankruptcy got caught stuffing themselves with
financial bonbons for their management skills only a few weeks
before they tried to stiff the company's creditors and employees.
When they were forced to return the goodies the Eaton boys
were lauded for their breeding and *noblesse oblige*.

EATON CENTRE, TORONTO
Plague Mall #1 and downtown Toronto's architectural wonder:
the fountains don't work, Michael Snow's Canada Geese don't
fly south, and you can't buy anything you can't get at any of 500
other malls in Canada.

ECONOMIC BRAIN TRUSTS
a) probably a contradiction in terms, given their dismal
   track record for predicting the way the Canadian economy is going to go;
b) well-heeled propaganda agencies and media lobbies set
   up to pressure governments and misinform the public to
   ensure that the rich, powerful and privileged remain (or
   lately, become more) rich, powerful and privileged;
c) if left-of-centre, college professors and trade union orga-
   nizers with unlimited faculty photocopy privileges and
   downtown mailboxes.
   See APEC, *Boards of Trade, Canadian Centre for Policy*

Alternatives, C.D. Howe Institute, Conference Board of Canada, Fraser Institute

ECONOMIC POLICY

A term that is never truthfully preceded by the word "coherent", and only very, very rarely by the words "sensible" or "sensitive", either in Canada or elsewhere.

ECONOMIC STABILITY

Secure loans and other forms of public debt for the offshore lending sector and their bond-raters.

A BRIEF SERMON ON ECONOMICS

The *Oxford Etymological Dictionary* tells us that the word *Economics* is rooted in household management and that its concerns logically ought to be intimate with those of ecology, which springs from the same etymological ground. The hodgepodge of definitions in the *Oxford English Dictionary* affirms this, tracing the word back to the confessions of John Gower in 1393, a man who believed in harmony, harvest and godly housekeeping. But by the 19th century economics had widened the scope from mere custodial tillage to the glamourized pretences of science, now purporting to examine that which relates "to the production and distribution of material wealth".

As Canada approaches the millennium economics has become less a practical arena than an ideological one, and needs to be sharply distinguished from commerce, which is the necessary but lower-case human activity of exchanging goods and services. Without commerce we'd all be sitting on the curb with parched faces wondering where our next meal is to come from. Without economics—as currently professed—we'd be no more confused than we are, and probably a little better informed on specifics. Neither economics nor commerce should be confused with finance, which is about manipulating money.

In a sane country, economics and finance would be sub-elements of the commercial system. Economists would offer common sense advice and encouragement to the productive economy, while counseling restraint to the sleazy impulses of those in the financial sector. Finance would play a larger but wholly pragmatic role as the Commonwealth's grease monkey, an instrumentation aimed at making optimum commercial performance easier for all.

That doesn't describe Canada, nor any other industrialized state. For us, economic theory has become the primary political arena, devouring politics, culture and common sense as it lurches toward totality. The seventy year struggle between Western capitalism and Soviet-style Marxism (which was a coconspiracy to narrow the definition of wealth and its distribution to nuclear warhead and delivery system counts) systematically rooted out and exterminated local culture all over the world. It was a struggle that should have ended with the unexpected and complete collapse of the Soviet empire in 1989. It didn't because capitalism is a growth- and conflict-based system, and when its evil twin collapsed, it simply flew out of control and invaded the intellectual systems that once nurtured it. Economics has become the vocabulary that defines nearly everything we now do and think, which is to say, it writes our political, social and cultural agendas, and defines most of our spiritual, intellectual and interpersonal parameters. We've become a society of asset calculators, whether we're buying groceries, watching a baseball game, having sex, or trying to save the planet from our greed and stupidity. It's one thing to use economics jargon when we're shopping for groceries, but when we begin to talk about our favourite baseball team's failure to capitalize on their opponent's mistakes, or think about equitable orgasm balances in the bedroom, we're not talking household management, we're going collectively and individually crazy.

EDMONTON

Former provincial capital and site of recent econopolitical experiments in refugee creation and culture-zapping. The attempts of Peter Pocklington and the Brothers Ghermezian to have the city's public assets deeded to them through government grants, tax giveaways and outright gifts have been only partly successful. Edmonton's right wing media alumni occupy key positions across the, er, Thomson and Hollinger newspaper chains.

WEST EDMONTON MALL

Alberta Plague Mall, or Disneyland North. Bad enough that the last 16,000 Saskatchewan wheat farmers winter on the wavepool's concrete beach like maggots on a breadboard while the wave machine drowns their children. This is the mall where you can get everything you never really wanted, and see nearly everything you never asked to see. If it weren't sucking the cultural lifeblood out of Edmonton, the zoo, the wave pool, NHL-size skating rink, indoor amusement park and the Fantasyland Hotel would be hilarious. Then you remember that this is what Ralph Klein and a majority of Albertans hope the future will be like.

EDUCATIONAL TELEVISION

Aside from being an obvious oxymoron, ET was a series of underfunded provincial television semi-networks that offered underproduced education programming to elementary and high school teachers too lazy or stupid to engage students on their own. For a few years it looked like it would become the vehicle for a nasty outbreak of long-distance education, but it is now in the process of being closed down and sold off to Moses Znaimer on the grounds that it has been made superfluous by U.S.-based cable network specialty channels. The disappearance of Canada's public television networks—whatever the budgetary excuses cited—is ideological and will set the cause of Canadian cultural independence back fifty years.

ATOM EGOYAN

If he wasn't little and bespectacled, from downtown Toronto, slightly weird and very WEWAP, he wouldn't have survived the earnest experimentality of his first films. But like anyone with intelligence who gets to practise a craft, he's grown. His 1995 film, *Exotica*, has a creepy, kinky, authentic explication of desire that distinguishes it from Hollywood film-making and makes it a more interesting enterprise than most CanLit or Can-Film. Chalk up another one to government subsidies to the arts. See WEWAP

ELLIOT LAKE

Secret radioactive sulfuric acid-laced water body created by massive debris from Canadian uranium mines. So why are the elderly being sent there to live on its shores?

MICHAEL ENRIGHT

Peter Gzowski's replacement at the CBC. Enright is a journalist and a public intellectual with strong values, a temper and a sense of humour. Gzowski was an entertainer.

ENTERTAINMENT INDUSTRY

The effective control sector of Media and communications in Canada, including, increasingly, what passes for news gathering and dissemination. The entertainment industry, in turn, is controlled by public relations directors, who see the new world in terms of infotainment, infomercials and controlled output. The disappearance, in other words, of editors and editorial independence. The Canadian entertainment industry is *not* headquartered within Canada's borders, despite all those nationally televised testimonials at media galas.

ENTREPRENEURS

Economic enter-and-take enthusiasts, popularized as culture heroes during the Reagan/Thatcher era and now, generally,

Neodarwinism's darlings and the supposed answer to everything that falls through the gaping holes in the global economy. Today's governments and corporations use entrepreneurs the way Adolf Hitler used his storm troopers: heavily dosed with propaganda, dazzled with showy medals and perks and then sacrificed in reverse order to their rank, power and value to the Reich when things don't go as planned. The wisdom of making opportunism a societal virtue is open to serious question.

ARTHUR ERICKSON

Semi-retired Vancouver architect who tried to reclaim modernism from its economic single-mindedness. He failed, but it was an interesting failure. Erickson is famous for his inattention to detail, particularly when it involves glass canopies. Rumours about Erickson are almost never true, despite being entertaining and quite probably self-generated.

ESKIMOS

a) obsolete shorthand for native tribes pushed beyond the treeline by 17th and 18th century migrations of Cree and Dogrib Indian militias;

b) western Inuit who haven't been driven to suicide by white cultural entrepreneurs trying to correct them in the Inuit language, which they don't speak;

c) Edmonton football team in the Confused Football League.

EUTHANASIA

Not the human species' greatest idea, but given world population levels, a better one than being born-again every time you go bankrupt or suffer a career setback. A couple of years ago dying B.C. resident Sue Rodriguez, suffering from ALS, went to the Canadian Supreme Court seeking a ruling in favour of assisted suicide. Instead she received a theological dissertation officially denying her permission to experience death-with-dignity in the name of "the sacredness of life". Not to suggest that life isn't sacred in this country, but there are some mornings when it looks like the ancient Greeks, who muttered "Best of all not to have been born", got it right. Telling people like Sue Rodriguez to have a nice day would qualify as what the Greeks called "hubris", or excessive pride in one's understanding of things.

PATERSON EWEN
Canada's greatest living painter and power tool enthusiast.

EXPATRIATE AMERICANS
Most of Canada's cultural entrepreneurs and officials are expatriate Americans who arrived in Canada seeking sanctuary from the Vietnam War and other asshole American behaviours. Nationalists tend to whine a lot about the presence of these Americans, who are frequently better Canadians than native-born Canadians, most of whom want to live at Disney World.

EXPLOSIVES
Supposedly not of interest to peaceful Canadians. Notwithstanding Bill C68 and the official policies of several political parties, do Canadians need the right to manufacture, carry and explode incendiary devices in public places (cf. Tim McVeigh, the Montana/Alberta militia, Reform Party, etc.)?

EXPO 67

"Man and His World", which opened in Montreal in the summer of 1967, was supposed to celebrate Canada's 100th birthday but actually marked the beginning of Montreal's decline as a Canadian and international centre. This happened partly because French Canadians noticed that the men involved spoke English, women realized that they didn't have much of a world to work with, and the offshore visitors recognized that Canada most resembled a plump white rabbit ready for skinning. Montreal's nine year downhill run as a "world class city" ended in the 1976 Olympics and a sea of red ink. See *world class*

EXPO 86

Trade Fair held in Vancouver, B.C. to celebrate the city's ascension to "world class" status. After four months of ridiculously expensive nightly fireworks displays, promises of future real estate profits and an entrepreneurial nirvana, the fair closed without coming through on a single one of its promises. Most of the site ended up in the hands of offshore real estate warlords after a cleanup of toxins that cost far more than the government got for the land; the B.C. economy (once the fog of prosperity created by injections of capital brought in from immigrant entrepreneurs and the drug trade lifts) is a third-world-type shambles; most of Vancouver's real estate is owned by Hong Kong interests; and the only new jobs the fair produced involved mopping up the red ink.

EXPORTS

The economic indicator by which, officially and erroneously, we judge the health of the economy. In a resource-based economy, exports are simply a measure of how fast the resources are being sucked out. And incidentally, Canada would be a net importer without the Auto Pact. Doesn't that make you suspicious? Given that the U.S. is either exploiting us or ordering us around in literally every other sector of the economy and political/cultural arena, why are we being allowed to get our yah-yahs with the Auto Pact?

FEDERALISM

Belief once widely held in Canada that a national government ought to have the determination, programs and constitutional powers to defend its citizens from noxious foreign manipulation and bullying, and their own laziness, stupidity and vile personal ambitions. Is that old-fashioned and silly? Just the people who've been defending federalism, apparently.

FESTIVAL CULTURE

Like most Western countries with an overabundance of trained professionals looking for markets to exploit, Canada has come under assault by frolic entrepreneurs who market celebrations without joy, pleasure without risk, mirth without the alcohol, drugs and sex that used to make it fun. These joyless professional merry-makers have already turned New Year's Eve into an electronically enhanced version of a Roman Bacchanalia—as conceived by daycare workers—and they're determined to bury every public spontaneity we have left beneath a denatured pall of commercially viable "fun".

FIGURE SKATERS

Oh, why not admit what we all know: Figure skating is the official Olympic sport of the gay community. That this is common knowledge and that one million Canadians will watch *any* televised figure skating event television networks run probably testifies more accurately to the degree of preconscious acceptance of homosexuality than the more official legal bench-marks sought by gay activists.

FINANCE

Within the banking sector, "finance" is the practice of lending large amounts of money to anyone willing to pay the interest charges—unless they are Canadian citizens and small business owners. For governments, "finance" means squeezing taxpayers, selling our grandchildren's birthright or borrowing to maintain a minimum level of security for citizens who don't need it. New Conservatives would like financial dithering to replace everything else we're interested in as the official culture of Canada. Finance is not to be confused with meaningful commercial activities, which involve capital investment in physical machinery, and hiring workers, something any financial expert will warn against.

TIMOTHY FINDLEY

Former actor, now avid gardener who is Canada's most revered homosexual chronicler of Rosedale, particularly for those who prefer their revered homosexuals not to write about their homosexuality. Findley writes novels, recently of decreasing quality and increased floridity.

FIRA

Foreign Investment Review Agency, set up by Trudeau to screen the nature and wisdom of incoming foreign capital. Trudeau believed that investment in industrial production was a good idea, but that incoming capital aimed at buying up existing industries and diverting profits out of the country wasn't. This agency, never very aggressive, was quickly defanged under Mulroney, and is now called Investment Canada. It consists of two overpaid clerks with wide grins on their faces and rubber stamps in their hands.

FIREWORKS

The annual fireworks festivals in major Canadian cities draw larger crowds than any other cultural or sporting events. As the global economy sinks us deeper into the Third World, expect these crowds to grow larger. West coasters explode private fireworks only on Halloween, Easterners on May 24th and July 1st. Albertans simply fire their guns into the air whenever they damned well please or whenever they hear French being spoken.

FIRST NATIONS (originally)

Canadian euphemism for pre-European wave of immigrants who were forced to stay drunk for five generations while governments and various religious organizations stole their land, eradicated their cultures and abused their children.

FIRST NATIONS (as evolved)

First, wakefulness and a rediscovered sobriety. Second, mandatory Oka-style dress for anyone under forty. Third, Chief Joseph-style public rhetoric. Eventual goal: real estate.

FISHERIES

A federal Cabinet post given only to politicians dedicated to the eradication of all marine and aquatic life in and around Canada. Now usually combined with Environment, Forestry or whatever else the federal Cabinet has decided is too far from Ottawa to be taken seriously.

FLEXIBILITY

A government procedure that replaced long range planning in Canada somewhere between 1975 and 1985. It means "responding to the results of the latest political poll", or "finding ways to screw and be screwed without removing one's dark blue business suit or betraying visible pleasure".

STEVE FONYO

Person-of-one-leg who hopped across Canada in 1984-85. Unlike Terry Fox (who was probably at least a third as nice as the media made him out to be, thus placing him above the Buddha and just below Jesus Christ), Fonyo drank, swore, was prone to outbursts of temper and ended up on the nasty end of several misdemeanor charges. He's living somewhere in Canada as a relatively normal, not always likeable human being nobody in the media ever wants to hear from again. That makes us forget that he was a courageous young man with an immense drive, and that we owe him a back-handed debt of gratitude for saving us from having our highways clogged with asymmetrical self-realizing pilgrims on what would inevitably have been increasingly bizarre personal quests for recognition and funds.

FOREIGN POLICIES

Independent Canadian ideas about the rest of the world, and about as common as hen's teeth. From Confederation until the end of WW II, Canadian foreign policy was dictated by the British Foreign Office. For a short period after WW II until the cancellation of the Avro Arrow by John Diefenbaker in 1959 and the related Bomark missile debacle in 1960, Canada practised a relatively independent military policy, and may have had one or two independent ideas about how to treat the rest of the world. In the 1990s, Canada's foreign policy consists of FTA, NAFTA and a general willingness to lie down and moan convincingly whenever NATO, GATT, the IMF/World Bank or the U.S. State Department feel the urge.

FORESTS

Once a renewable resource, but with Canada's massive overcutting and the universal failure to replant it is probably more accurate to call them pre-tundra.

FORESTS FOREVER

A corporate publicity program in British Columbia inspired by the "Wise Use" anti-environmental movement in the U.S. and designed to convince Canadians and offshore watchdog groups that B.C.'s forest industry is on a sustained yield basis. It has spawned a series of small-town red-neck sub-cells across B.C. called, somewhat ironically, "Share B.C.", which argue that forestry conservation is a communist plot mounted by feminists and homosexuals against the 200 or so hard-working loggers still working the forests. The success of "Forests Forever" and its subsidiary organizations has been considerable—but hardly surprising given that the annual publicity budgets rival the entire budget of the Forest Service.

FORKED TONGUES

Speech and cognitive disorder contracted by many Native Indian leaders while trying to outsmart white politicians. Easily identified by the absence of laughter.

DAVID FOSTER

Musical arranger and producer frequently cited as an example of what Canadians can do in the international culture market: produce overblown musical puddings so heavily crusted with electric violins and other technomusical sentimentalities that suicidal secretaries can be sent over the edge after only eight or ten bars. Foster is the Lawrence Welk of the 1990s.

TERRY FOX

B.C. resident who lost a leg to bone cancer in 1977 and conceived the truly nutty idea of hippety-hopping from coast to coast to draw attention to inadequate cancer research funding. He gave up in Northern Ontario in 1981 when the cancer metastasized. After his death he became a national and international symbol of, er, continued inadequate funding for cancer research.

DIANE FRANCIS

Maclean's magazine columnist, *Financial Post* editor and professional media cheerleader-of-choice whenever a right wing government does something cruel or stupidly ideological enough to require media justification. Francis' basic line is always the same: *You aren't being nearly cruel and stupid enough to inspire investor confidence*. Her recent tome on what English Canada ought to do to Quebec made Lucien Bouchard's political narcissism seem positively moderate by comparison.

FRANK MAGAZINE

Ottawa's answer to our national deficit of nasty gossip. *Frank's* main weakness, aside from a financially inspired disinclination to investigate anything, is that it can't decide whether it wants to be Britain's *Private Eye* magazine, *Spy* or *The National Enquirer*. Still, any magazine that has so many enemies in high places must be doing something right, and it is the only public instrument in the country that isn't totally cowed by the threat of libel chill.

FRASER INSTITUTE

Well-heeled West Coast think-tank filled to bursting with monetarist enthusiasts bent on creating a new generation of homophobic reactionaries. Its supporting clientele tends to be corporations or eighty year olds who are legal wards of the Reform Party. The Fraser Institute is easy to ridicule, but the truth is that it has more political energy and organizational talent than the entire left side of the political spectrum in Canada. It ought to be taken very, very, seriously by anyone who doesn't want to see us all end up clouting one another with 2x4s.

THE FRASER VALLEY

Richest stretch of former farmland on the West Coast now being Wise Use-d into bedroom communities for Vancouver's service

industries and pockmarked with Bible-thumping enclaves of
fundamentalists who have seen Jesus and can't distinguish him
from Preston Manning. Fraser Institute executives do not live in
the Fraser Valley.

FREE TRADE

Code term for a vague plan to make life easier for financial sector
personnel and nasty, brutish and short for everyone else. In practice, Free Trade has involved dropping financial, cultural and
trade protections against the U.S. without asking for anything in
return. Whether this tactic was motivated by Brian Mulroney's
stupidity or his lifelong neurotic desire to lick U.S. political and
corporate Gucci loafers is still unclear—unlike the equally
loathsome effects of the agreements his government signed.

FTA

Acronym for 1988 political/cultural agreement between Canada
and the U.S. aimed at providing executives and other technical
functionaries of the multinational corporate sector with dual citizenship and guaranteed rights to taxation-free profits in both
countries. Subsidiary elements of the formal Agreement in-
cluded the right of Canada to retain higher levels of social entitlement and cultural funding without the financial means to
sustain either and the orderly and staged erosion of Canada's
industrial base and socio-cultural institutions under the euphemism of "harmonization of programs and standards". The
U.S. obtained the right to continue trade harassment without
remedy or reason, even though it was not required to provide
compensatory climate control within Canadian cities unable to

protect the newly equivalent Canadian homeless sector against Canada's harsher winters.

FRESH WATER

Canada has over 100,000 cubic metres of fresh water available each year to every one of its citizens. By comparison, Libya has 160.

Why aren't we cleaner?

Why do we want to drink imported beer and designer water from France?

Why aren't we more worried about being invaded by thirsty Californian suburbanites—or by Libyans?

BARBARA FRUM

The late host of "The Journal", CBC's ultraplush national news program of the 1980s. Frum turned into a giggling teenager whenever confronting major international political figures, and was locally famous for having a clothing budget roughly equivalent to the network's budget for foreign correspondents. Her untimely death in 1992 has been used as a rationale for Cabinet initiatives aimed at disbanding CBC's news-gathering apparatus in favour of using the various collapsing U.S. newsgathering networks. Frum's reputation as an interviewer has been enhanced by the behaviour of her successors. No one is quite sure who is to blame for the behaviour of her children.

DAVID FRUM

Quintessential aggrieved white guy and grimacing post-teen right-wing hepcat who thinks that social services are character corrupting. Best argument going that smacking your children when they misbehave ought to be reconsidered.

NORTHROP FRYE

Speed typist and biblical scholar whose articulate belief in literature as the gestural zone of polite middle-class amateurs normally incapable of gestures made him, for a time, the Bob White of University English professors across Canada. His opus, while not toxic in and of itself, has led to a functional separation between those who create literature and those who process it for industrial reasons, and has virtually ended any serious study of domestic literature in the country. Unless it involved Marshall McLuhan, whose centre at the University of Toronto Frye was reputed obsessed with crushing, the Great Professor was an extremely decent and witty man. But isn't that what he should have been, given the degree of respect and privilege he was accorded?

ROBERT FULFORD

Radio critic recently resurrected by the media to represent the elderly and the four-square-behind-the-Family Compact, Fulford may be the only old guy in the country's intelligensia who hasn't lost his stuff. Fulford bears a close physical resemblance to Mr. Weatherbee from the old Archie comic books, and critiques accordingly most of the time. That's a shame, because he has a highly entertaining mean streak. Despite appearances, he is *not* a conservative intellectual or an aggrieved white guy.

FUNDING AGENCIES

Current Canadian governments claim at every level that Canadians can't continue to expect cultural funding from the public sector and that artists should learn to beg from the corporate sector. But so long as the corporate sector is a bunch of foreign-owned branch plants, alternate funding has roughly the chance of a snowball in hell. The corporations are here to suck profits out of the country, not redistribute them to us, and they've made it clear that if they want to hear the natives playing violins, they'll wait till they're working the street corners with a monkey and a tin cup. So bring on the next set of phony alternatives to government funding.

GALIANO ISLAND
B.C. Gulf island and Lesbos West. The only place in Canada outside of the Queen Charlotte Islands that has customs checks at the ferry terminal. Those not wearing Birkenstock sandals are ridiculed and given vitamin enemas, then deported. Competes with nearby Saltspring Island as the least hospitable spot in Canada.

HANA GARTNER
CBC person-of-news. Don't you wish she'd get a new earring consultant, and stop smirking while she's explaining why so many women and children have died in Bosnia? Gartner is living proof that it's *not* hard to get by just upon a smile and that editorial depth on television *is* an oxymoron.

GASPE
Area of patriotic pride for French Canadians, and occasional site of experimental mass chemotherapy, hence the name.

Uninhabitable to all mammals but nature photographers and a shrinking population of diseased whales and fur seals.

GEMINIS
Canada's awards for television merit—thousands and thousands of them despite the scarcity of watchable television programming. Until recently, the only television people who had time to watch or vote on the awards were CBC's thousands and thousands of non-producing producers. With them gone or soon to be departing, expect stranger but more entertaining events to happen at the ceremonies. Perhaps even a host whose name isn't Albert Schultz.

GENERALS (RETIRED)
After Lewis MacKenzie became a media star by accomplishing absolutely nothing as head of U.N. peace-keeping forces in Bosnia in the early 1990s, the goal of Canadian military personnel changed from "serve and protect" to "screw up outside the country but give first rate interviews to CNN, retire immediately and sign a book deal, become a television commentator whenever two or more olive-garbed human beings begin to hack at or shoot one another, and run for parliament under the banner of most opportunistic political party". Due to some miscalculations on the part of MacKenzie's advisors, Canadian civilians have been spared from having the general conduct his moral renaissance from the floor of the House of Commons. The bad news is that if the Somalia Inquiry achieves what it ought to and roots out the corruption in the armed forces, there won't be anyone left in the Canadian Armed Forces with a rank higher than

master sergeant, and the retired generals will form an entire new lunatic fringe political party.

GENIES

Awards given to Canadian filmmakers after stuffing them with rubber chicken. We make films, but FTA and NAFTA took away any hope of distributing them. Why not skip the chicken and submit everything directly to Jack Valenti? See *CanFilm*

THE GLOBE & MAIL

"Canada's Newspaper" in the sense that it is not terribly well written, isn't terribly well edited or managed, isn't politically independent of foreign control, and, well, isn't very Canadian. Tends to choose soup-makers as top executives, right wing Edmonton philosophers as editors and privatization as the best option for everything.

GLENN GOULD

Amateur Stockbroker. Good pianist. Strange person. Subject for innumerable CBC radio documentaries. ZZZZZZZZZ. . . .

GOVERNMENT/INDUSTRY COOPERATION

Code word for bizarre economic development practice nearly universal among Canadian governments:

a) Governments sign into cooperative ventures with large, financially plump corporations (preferably foreign-owned or controlled), and pump vast numbers of dollars into goofy joint ventures in the form of direct grants, tax credits or non-secured loans.

b) While the money input is near its peak, the corporations whine loudly about bureaucratic interference, high taxation and Big Government.

c) When and if the joint venture becomes profitable, the politicians privatize it, write off the public investment and offer the participating corporations further asset write-downs, tax credits and further grants until the corporation decides to close the in-country manufacturing facilities and move them to the U.S. or Mexico.

d) If (as is usually the case) the joint venture fails, the loans are written off, the tax grants forgiven, and the government leaders make *mea culpa* confessions about the dangers of socialism. Cf. the Bricklin car or growing cucumbers in Newfoundland.

GOVERNORS GENERAL

Ceremonial representatives of the British Crown, the post is now conferred upon political retirees who have demonstrated skills at standing still for long periods without mumbling or fainting during their active careers.

GEORGE GRANT

Canadian philosopher, author of *Technology and Empire*, a book that got nearly everything Marshall McLuhan missed or glossed over. Grant was not a "supermind" and his lack of recognition offers a credible argument that it isn't always a great idea to write clear sentences filled with connected, lucid ideas.

LORNE GREENE

Greene left the CBC in the late 1950s to become an American father figure on *Bonanza*, the last television program to argue that women are irrelevant and don't need to come on the cattle drive. Later on Greene worked as the only TV host ever to simulcast voice and his own unique interpretation of international sign language. While only 13 percent of Americans believe Elvis is still alive, 70 percent of Canadians believe that Greene is still alive and guiding U.S. network television from his isolated Arizona ranch.

ALLAN GREGG

Tory pollster and media *bon vivant*. If everyone systematically lied to people like Allan Gregg for about five years, the accuracy of the polls would disintegrate, the pollster's stranglehold on the Canadian political system would loosen, and we could start having political lives based on what ought to be done, not on our vilest and most myopic impulses.

WAYNE GRETZKY

Archetypal Canadian character, late 1970s, early 1980s. Slight, fast, married to an American movie starlet, more interested in sidelines than the main game, intensely loyal until something better shows up. Durable and not easily hit. "If you try to stop me, I'll pass to someone else, and he'll get what I want." Lives in Los Angeles, plays where the money is.

WALTER GRETZKY

Premier Canadian dad of the late 20th century.

PAUL GROSS

Television's proof that the RCMP is nicer, smarter and better groomed than America's peace officers—just in case there was anyone left in either country who didn't see the Rodney King videos or watch Mark Fuhrman during the O. J. Simpson trial. Gross was not sold to Disney with the RCMP image rights.

TWO GRUDGES THAT QUEBEC JUSTIFIABLY HOLDS AGAINST ENGLISH CANADA

a) Clarence Campbell's suspension of Rocket Richard in 1957. Montrealers busted up St. Laurent street, Les Canadiens lost the Stanley Cup, and Québécois are still steaming about it.

b) The Iroquois. The French backed the Hurons, the English helped the Iroquois exterminate them, and that's why there are no francophone Indians.

PETER GZOWSKI

Fuzzy-voiced CBC employee, talk-show host and nationalist astronaut personally charged with preserving national unity among the 5000 educated upper middle class English-speaking Canadians who listen to the CBC. His last few years were marked by a curious unwillingness to interview anyone smarter than he is, a phenomenon that made both the country and the CBC difficult to defend intelligently.

HACKERS AND HEWERS

Mythic Canadians devised and held onto by theme-obsessed historians and journalists who seem to have missed the fact that Canadian resource harvesting is now the most technologically advanced (read labour-free) on the planet. There are reputedly eighteen to twenty hackers and hewers in the woods north of Peterborough harvesting scrub hardwoods for Toronto's wood-fired pizza ovens.

HALLOWEEN

The Night of Misrule was once the single annual occasion in Canada when small children were permitted to make themselves sick eating candy and adolescents were allowed to settle scores with grumpy adults and test pipe bombs, the tensile strength of egg shells and other minor IRA ordnance. Now a night of social terror controlled by apple/razor perverts and UNICEF do-gooders.

DAVID HALTON

Attenuated strain of Canadian television journalism. Despite his pedigree, this guy is to news reporting what Zamfir is to classical music. Zamfir is okay if you're on Valium, but television is already a neural tranquilizer.

GERALD HANNON

Middle-aged homosexual journalist, part-time Ryerson professor, part-time father-figure prostitute who periodically disturbs the public calm by trying to be a living demonstration that the marketplace can accommodate anyone and anything—and thus raise the hackles of fundamentalists of nearly every dispensation, including the gay community.

OFRA HARNOY

Cellist and the all-round fool-destroying blonde bombshell everybody hoped Liona Boyd might grow up to be.

ELIJAH HARPER

Native Indian MPP from Manitoba who stopped Meech Lake with an eagle feather and many repetitions of the word "no". He's probably also the most interesting guy anywhere in Canada to go fishing for Northern Pike with.

MICHAEL HARRIS

Golf dufus and lead thinker, after Newt Gingrich, in Ontario's Common Sense Revolution. Harris will be the most hated man in Canada by the year 2000 for his Marie Antoinette social policies. His attempts to appear thoughtful in television commercials are among the several truly hilarious regular events in Canadian media. Last book read was *Mr. Silly* by Roger Hargreaves. Check the book out of the library if you're curious to know what kind of thought entertains late 20th Century conservative premiers. . . .

HEALTH AND DOCTORS

There's no necessary relation between these two things any more. We merely live longer, and the doctors employ every known medical device except nurses, hospitals and timely surgeries to ensure that we do. In the next few years these two words are likely to be associated with things like *private health insurance, decline of medical coverage, closure of hospitals, jettisoning of nurses,* and *user fees.*

PRIVATE HEALTH INSURANCE

Watch for the proliferation of companies selling this commodity in the next few years. While our governments continue to insist that universal medical care is a basic Canadian right, the individual provinces continue to shed medical procedures they're willing to pay for until your UMC will cover nothing more than a biannual medical exam to find out if you're suffering from cholera, yellow fever, beriberi and whooping cough. Vaccines for these afflictions will be available at Walmart for a nominal charge.

PETER HERRNDORF

Toronto cocktail circuit schmooze-meister and self-appointed spokesperson for Public Broadcasting noted for defending public institutions in the 1990s with the values and slogans of the 1960s. Currently overseeing the collapse and demise of the CBC and TVO, Ontario's educational television network. Has an extremely wealthy sister, which probably helps to explain some of his career decisions more easily than he could.

HISTORY

Canada has a deceptively interesting history, almost none of which is discussed or even referenced in this dictionary. That is not because the past isn't important or relevant, or because I'm one of those media airheads who thinks human history commenced with the first network television broadcast, but because I didn't want this dictionary to be the size of Rohinton Mistry's last novel. Hence, I've narrowed my historical focus to those ciphers that seem implicated in the deception and lies I want to combat.

HOCKEY

Game of choice for semi-literate male cement-heads that supposedly reveals the Canadian national character: young men dressed in plastic-reinforced polyester suits sliding around on sheets of ice at blinding speeds chasing a disk of circular black rubber, slashing themselves and imported Europeans with aluminum-fibreglass weapons, and punching one another in the face at the slightest provocation. Until recently, the management and marketing of the sport has been the most incompetent in the history of professional or amateur sport, and the players union was operated as a divine right monarchy by a man who once tried to start a nuclear war with the Soviet Union during a tournament game in Moscow. The anomalies in the game's bleak history have been the occasional presence of Ken Dryden as an analyst and Ron McLean as a commentator, along with the fact that the game is of no intrinsic interest to the United States, notwithstanding the recent flight of franchises southward.

MINOR HOCKEY

It's hard to say how this came about, but between the homophobes, the media's Reptile Machine and the caring professionals who want to make us afraid of everybody and everything, we've managed to make minor hockey and daycare centres the two leading public stewpots of child molesters. Well, everybody is for apprehending and punishing molesters, but all this publicity shouldn't be taken to mean that parents no longer need to teach their kids not to go into dark, enclosed spaces with members of certain occupational groups we've all known since about 1497 were prone to attract molesters.

HOLLINGER
Owned by long-winded Canadian communications mogul Conrad Black, who's out to prove he's better at downsizing than anyone in the industry, as Saskatchewan's newspapers discovered a year or two back, and many more newspapers are soon to discover. Now controls 58 percent of Canada's print media.

KARLA HOMOLKA
Jailed sex killer who was the gasoline for Paul Bernardo's rapist-as-entrepreneur engine. The easy way to deal with this woman is to whine that she wasn't adequately punished, and campaign for stiffer sentences for criminals. But a more relevant response might be to have a close look inside her Disney-icon-besplattered jail cell, which gives us a chilling glimpse of our fate if Mickey Mouse and the global economy succeeds in replacing culture and civility with sentimental greed, aggressive self-absorption and the universal consumer shopping mall.

C. D. HOWE INSTITUTE
Named after C. D. Howe, who went bankrupt building grain elevators in the 1930s, and later pioneered government/industry

cooperation in 1956, building pipelines that transported oil and funnelled public funds into corporate pockets. The C. D. Howe Institute surfaced in 1973, and is fond of accusing the Canada Pension Plan of being a pyramid scheme while insisting that the stock market and private sector banks aren't. . . .

GORDIE HOWE
Archetypal Canadian, 1950s and 60s: shy, slope-shouldered, large. Wife interested in money, but Howe liked hockey more than anything else. Great stamina and elbows. "I'll stop you and break some bones if you try to get around me, and then I'll score enough goals to win and get what my wife wants."

HUMAN RESOURCES
Euphemism for surplus persons. Until the last decade, surplus persons were officially thought of as unemployed or as students studying obsolete subjects in universities and trade schools. This same resource is now mainly being deported from province to province as welfare rates are ratchetted downward and entitlement criteria are made more onerous.

IMMIGRATION POLICY
A cynical view of recent Canadian immigration policy would describe it as a mechanism originally designed to get the dishes washed in fast food chains that devolved into a system willing to let anyone wealthy enough buy their way into the country.

It's much more complicated than that. Since the 1950s Canada has had no coherent or stable immigration policy, but rather a series of bureaucratic capitulations to circumstance mixed with political collapses in the face of expedience which together have resulted in one unfortunate ruling after another.

What the solutions to the mess of immigration are isn't very clear to anyone, but some of the unadmitted effects are:

a) a patchwork set of entrance regulations based primarily on the worst sort of nepotism or on the principle of receiverless bribes;

b) the presence of several xenophobic and openly racist immigrant minorities in various parts of the country, some of them organized and militant, others simply wealthy enough to buy whatever tolerance or fear best serves them;

c) a serious split between the major urban centres, which are multicultural and in several locations dominantly non-European, and the hinterlands, which are white and getting hostile about it;

d) neither the will nor any effective mechanisms to introduce incoming immigrants to the culture of Canada. Today's immigrants are invited to bring their habitations with them, lock, stock and barrel, even when they are refugees coming from dysfunctional cultures that have degenerated into barbarism and violence.

IMPORTS

Imports are forbidden by theoretical economists as fruit of the devil—unless it is investment capital or is being brought in for direct use by the theoretical economists, funding agencies and other affiliated corporate officials, together with their friends and families.

INDEPENDENT WEEKLIES

Mostly a carryover of what used to be called underground news-papers such as Toronto's *Now* magazine, and Vancouver's *Georgia Straight*, they are 70 percent entertainment industry non-news and 20 percent ideological clichés that we'll all be embarrassed about within five years. But the other 10 percent will be the only non-corporate political and cultural analysis available to casual readers in Canada's big cities, and that makes them pretty damned important. See *weeklies*

INDUSTRIAL RESOURCES

Once significant in volume and sited mainly in Ontario and parts of Quebec. Currently on their way to Mexican *Maquili-doros* on American-owned transport trucks.

HAROLD INNIS

1950s University of Toronto academic who wrote several brilliant essays on the fur trade to which he appended some tentative speculations about the need for efficient lines of communication north of the 49th parallel if Canada was to thrive economically and in other ways. Innis' untimely death in 1953 has resulted in generations of subsequent academic intellectual embroidery, blather, self-serving enthusiasms and other genial miscommunication. Innis is still a regular invitee to Liberal Party culture wanks.

INTELLECTUALS

Canada has about 800 of these fragile devices, 90 percent of whom know one another but never talk freely except at conferences. Not to be confused with university professors or members of the media, who are not intellectuals and never talk freely about anything, least of all at conferences.

CONSERVATIVE INTELLECTUALS

Conservative intellectuals would like to return Canadian society to the late 19th Century, particularly to its poorhouses, picturesquely starving children and regular whippings for the recalcitrant and uncooperative amongst the servant classes. Not necessarily members of conservative political parties or employees of the *Globe & Mail* or Conrad Black, but most of them are as chubby-faced as Black. Makes you wonder what they're eating for breakfast, don't it? See *aggrieved white guys*

INTERNET

The digital version of open mouth radio, soon to become the digital equivalent of those advertising flyers that clog your mailbox. If this is the Information Highway, let's blow up the bridges and ramps before it's too late.

INUIT

One-time Eskimos in the Eastern Arctic attempting to gain restitution for ecological and cultural trauma of incoming nature photographers through self-government, cultural self-deification and six-month annual government-paid vacations for Native population in global funspots.

INVESTOR CONFIDENCE

A new and mysterious need of wealthy people and lending agencies to have their confidence constantly and egregiously bolstered by government tax breaks, policy wonks, and cruel treatment of persons with low incomes. This need is not uniquely Canadian, but it may put an end to Canada.

JANE JACOBS

American-born urban critic and scholar who settled in Toronto during the Vietnam War to protect her children and her sanity. She has become a national treasure, and a beacon to U.S.-born immigrants for her commitment to and understanding of the differences between local and cosmopolitan values, and how they rarely have any resemblance to government policies and urban development practices. See *Amer-Canadians*

GRAHAM JAMES

Hockey coach, properly convicted molester, prison inmate. That being said, a query is in order: It's easy to accept that it was sexual assault the first 150 times, but what about the second 150 times? At some point doesn't complicity and preference become an issue, or are we having too damned much fun catching and burning witches to care?

JAMES BAY I

Hydroelectric development designed to drown Northern Quebec's native and caribou populations while providing separatist Québécois with economic dowry for entry into the North East Power Grid. Primary drownee to date is Quebec Government, in red ink.

JAMES BAY II

Indian lands, if Quebec attempts to separate from Canada.

JAPANESE RESTAURANTS

One of the pleasures of Vancouver is that it has the best Japanese restaurants in North America, and the only good ones in Canada. It's enough to make you miss the place if you've left it.

JE ME SOUVIENS

Quebec's licence plate slogan. Freely translated, it means, "*You English peegs may have defeated Montcalm on the Plains of Abraham, but we're going to get you back if we have to destroy Quebec and Canada to do it.*" So much for the most benign 230 year military occupation in human history.

JOBS

We don't seem to have enough jobs to go around, or governments that recognize that the lack of meaningful work is the primary threat to Canada, not a debt crisis that is nearly pure ideology. How can you have a just or happy society unless the abilities of its citizens are wanted?

BEN JOHNSON

Jamaican sprinter, steroid user, comeback artist. Was he a hoax or the victim of a hoax? Just exactly what was the hoax?

JULY 1st

Formerly Dominion Day, now Canada Day. It was more fun when we were still sure there was something to celebrate other than American domination and the availability (in Ontario) of poor quality Taiwanese fireworks.

JUNOS

Canadian Music Awards given to musical performers acceptable to parents. This explains why Anne Murray, Murray McLauchlin, Corey Hart and various friends of David Foster have basements filled with Juno trophies. Things are getting better, if you think Alanis Morissette is a step in the right direction.

KAREN KAIN

Aristocratic and once beautiful, now merely glamorous in an upper-class old-fashioned Canadian sort of way. If she'd come of age ten years earlier, married Glenn Gould instead of Ross Petty and had about five children, Canada would be a better place and Kain would have been an even more extraordinary dancer. Now condemned to doing farewell tours until she's well into her seventies.

JOANNE KATES

Toronto restaurant critic so secretive about her identity that even close associates won't admit privately she's really the snubbed Tory back-bencher and socialite Isabel Bassett. Being from Toronto, Kates wouldn't know a good Japanese restaurant from a semitrailer truck even if it backed its duals over her limousine.

MACKENZIE KING

Canadian prime minister 1935-51 who guided Canada through WW II by consulting with his dead mother and discussing economic and foreign policy with his dog, thus setting precedents for Prime Ministerial behaviours during the 1980s and 1990s.

KINGSTON
Beloved of Don Cherry, birthplace of Doug Gilmour, Kirk Muller and the Tragically Hip, site of Canada's major criminal holding tanks, point of origin for the *Harrowsmith* lifestyle, and home to every gardening writer west of the Rockies, most of whom have recently lost their jobs to corporate American buyouts, and are moonlighting as folksingers, lesbian therapists and prison guards.

W. P. KINSELLA
American writer and Indian fighter, but such a big fan of Canada's medicare system that he still resides in Canada. The Mulroney government elected him to the Order of Canada for his loyalty to Canadian values, and for believing that heaven is somewhere in Iowa. Kinsella writes (and writes and writes . . .) about baseball despite the handicap of only having handled a baseball for the purposes of having publicity photos taken.

RALPH KLEIN
Alberta premier, former open mouth radio host and all-round fiscal butt-kicker and opportunist. He became a corporate culture hero by exporting homeless and other disadvantaged Albertans to other provinces.

LABOUR
Depending on who's talking:
a) a vestigial element in capital accumulation;

b) the most heroic of victim classes and the source of all human virtues.

Nobody has ever been very clear about what labour is, but there's a popular belief circulating within the business community right now that in late 20th Century economies it has no purpose.

LABOUR DAY

End-of-summer holiday after which former workers head down to the UIC offices to discover that their entitlements have run out, and that they're no longer eligible for welfare either.

GUY LAFLEUR

Archetypal Canadian, 1970s. Fast, exciting to watch, but smokes cigarettes in the dressing-room, smashes up cars and only remembers his name two hours before gametime. "Try to stop me. See if I care." Indestructible, except from within. Lives in Montreal, and nobody can imagine him anywhere else until he leaves.

LAKES

Pre-reservoirs/or holding tanks for sewage and liquid industrial waste. In Eastern Canada outside the ground-pollutable areas, acid rain has lowered the pH balance in most lakes to levels that are lethal to fish and most other aquatic life-forms, but merely corrosive to human epidermis.

GREAT LAKES

Sewerways for Central Canadians, who like to pretend that the real pollution comes from Cleveland, Ohio, instead of the 500 or so miniature Clevelands that dot the northern shore of the lake system.

LAND CLAIMS

Native Indian program to overturn the treaties they signed— usually at gunpoint, while drunk or absent—between 1550 and late last week. Unfortunately, settling land claims will force Native Indians to become white real estate entrepreneurs and necessitate a new variety of absurdist theatre that enables those without cultural concepts of land ownership logical and dignified entrance to a collapsing culture that is entirely based on the ownership and division of property.

MICHELLE LANDSBERG

Stephen Lewis' wife, donut enthusiast and constant, high-pitched whiner. Once a gifted feminist journalist, the predictability of her views now serves as an example of why the New Conservative movement is ascendant.

k d LANG

Vegetarian entertainer and lesbian culture hero. She may or may not be the reincarnation of Patsy Cline, but she's literally everything Alberta's Klein government would like to eradicate.

SILKEN LAUMANN

Olympic power rower, drugstore spokesperson. She has Canada's healthiest gums. Her recent TV biography rendered everyone other than dental professionals unconscious within minutes.

IRVING LAYTON

Now-elderly Montreal poet, blowhard and self-declared Nobel Prize candidate with an over-eager "cowled friar" no Canadian woman has ever quite been willing to go on record as having actually seen.

JAMES LAXER

With Mel Watkins, the last NDP spokesguys for lost causes, labour sentimentalities, and a small, intermittent common sense.

STEPHEN LEACOCK

McGill university professor and Canadian Uncle Remus beloved of sentimental university professors and public sector broadcasters all across Canada. Recently replaced by Gordon Lightfoot as official tourism spokesperson for the City of Orillia, Ontario.

LOUISE LECAVALIER

Blonde dreadlocked principal dancer for Montreal's amazing LaLaLa Human Steps. She is—or was, now that her knees are gone—Canada's most stunning dancer, worth every cent Canada has pumped into Quebec culture. If this is the kind of product a distinct, heavily subsidized society produces, then give it more money.

PAMELA LEE

The most-recognized Canadian on the planet, even if no one knows she's a Canadian and her most distinguishing physical feature is American-made silicon.

SOOK YIN LEE

Western civilization's revenge on Chinese immigration, and vice versa. Will she end up as the next Adrienne Clarkson or as merely another in an endless string of revenges on conventional sexuality? By the time she's been fully reprocessed by Moses Znaimer's view of the universe, will anyone care?

LEGAL INFANTILIZATION

There's a statute in Ontario that says that if a woman doesn't receive independent legal counsel, any contract she signs under Family Law is null and void. Not to be a FACT advocate or anything, but is this really helping women, or just giving them another easement that cripples them?

MARIO LEMIEUX

Archetypal Canadian, late 1980s: oversized, bilingual, interested primarily in money, physically fragile. "If you try to stop me, I'll reach around you and get what I want anyway." Lives in the U.S. and retires young.

PETER LERAT

Toronto lunatic who, imitating the values of the corporate sector, held a variety of wild animals hostage on the streets of Toronto, demanding money from passersby before he would release them. Lerat was jailed for his behaviour, most of the animals he took hostage died of shock, while the corporate sector. . . .

RENE LEVESQUE

Short, balding, cigarette-smoking leftist Quebec political leader not to be confused with anyone in any major 1990s Quebec political movement. Lévesque wanted Quebec to separate from Canada because he believed that English Canada was getting all the bonbons, was suppressing Quebec culture and the French language—and that it would continue to do these things. As a result, Ottawa has had the bonbon hose down Quebec's throat ever since and Quebec culture has a better chance of surviving globalization, Disneyfication and the New Conservative movement than English Canada. Still, the ideas that energized René Lévesque have about as much to do with the Quebec separatism of the 1990s as Che Guevara's ideas about socialist revolution have to do with the Cuba of the 1990s. Quebec's current leadership seems determined to put a high percentage of Northern Quebec under water in order to gain membership to the U.S. Northeast Power Grid, and the leaders themselves want to take long paid vacations in Paris and New York under the pretence of attending G-7 and U.N. conferences.

STEPHEN LEWIS

Former Ontario NDP leader and socialite. Brian Mulroney appointed him to represent Canada at the U.N., thus demonstrating how liberal both men could be. Lewis is much respected in Ontario—or in downtown Toronto and Ottawa anyway. Outside Ontario people merely wonder why he talks like an Anglican bishop with lemon wedges crammed into each cheek. Ten years from now this will be an entry on his son Avie, who is a major mind at Much Music. (That isn't quite a contradiction in terms. Really.)

LIBEL CHILL

A set of legal maneuvers and moral intimidations more used in Canada than anywhere in the world outside of Disney to protect the solitude of the money-counting classes and to silence journalistic and artistic inquiry.

LIBERALS

Reactionary Conservatives who buy and hang the work of prominent Canadian visual artists in their homes and who are too lazy to get hot about their own reactions. Not to be confused with American liberals, who are extinct.

LIES

Canadians are neck-deep in lies. Lying about what's happening has become the only non-denominational activity all Canadians share. The lies come from our politics, our commercial system, our media and press. The lies come from the political right, where the power lies, but they're also coming from our fast-shrinking centre and left. The lies come from our collective and individual greed and intolerance, from our public and private myopia, and they come from an education system so overwhelmed with correctness-crazed safety freaks it's only willing to teach our kids to have a nice day. Some of the lies are planned and deliberate futurehype, others are designed to habituate us to products (or lately, to the absence and uneven distribution of product) and some are designed to overload and disable our critical faculties so more lies can be stuffed down our craws. These kinds of lies are a testament to the growing fear of democracy and openness that is the dark side of the information revolution we are experiencing. The more powerful the engine of lying, the greater the wastage and debris and polution.

ERIC LINDROS

Archetypal Canadian, 1990s: oversized, too aggressive, too interested in money, endurance questionable. "Get the fuck out of my way or I'll run over you." Resides in his mother's lap in suburban Toronto during the offseason when not getting into barfights.

STUDENT LOANS

Our governments encourage kids to mortgage their souls by running up forty grand in student loans, then demand that they pay back the loans six months after graduation even though the only jobs available for them are minimum wage service industry McJobs. When a few kids go south on the loans, the governments froth at the mouth about moral degeneracy and then, in what they propose to the media as a conciliatory gesture, extend the payback period a few months. The way we offer Latin American banana republics a better financial deal than we do our own children says more about our social investment priority than a dozen righteous ministers dithering over "quality of education" does.

LOBSTER SCANDAL

A 1980s incident, probably fictitious, in which federal fisheries attempted to stock several West Coast inlets with 140,000 juvenile Atlantic lobsters, but forgot to remove the elastic bands from their claws before releasing them. In the real world, the lobsters would have died of oxygen starvation on the plane coming from Nova Scotia when fisheries scientists stopped in Calgary to get drunk and chow down on some Alberta grain-fed porterhouse steaks.

LOGIC, APPLIED COMMERCIAL

If we've really created a secure continental marketplace with NAFTA, and have gained ready access to the global marketplace through GATT, and *if* capitalism reigns supreme and constitutes the only possible road to social and political justice; and *if* we're really concerned about excessive government—Can't we disband the Federal Trade Secretariat, fire the hordes of nattering government economists, tighten up the rules on non-profit societies to exclude political lobbies, close the industrial development cargo cults that now moulder at every level of government, and let capitalism do its work? Or are we missing something, or not being told what the downscaling and deregulation of government is really about, and for? Just asking. . . .

LONDON, ONT

The only city in the world where women are forced by civic ordinance to dress in Laura Ashley designer clothes. Populated mainly by insurance executives, accountants and visual artists, determined not to be mistaken for citizens of London, England, or anywhere else.

LOS ANGELES
California city Canadian media figures refuse to emigrate to—
unless offered work. Thought by unobservant actors and other
chronic optimists to be under the control of Lorne Greene,
Leslie Neilson and Wayne Gretzky. Most of the actors who move
there return home two years later with permanent tans, inflated
body parts and deflated bank accounts and egos.

LOTUSLAND
A term coined in the 1970s by former humourist Allan Fotheringham to describe the lifestyle of about 10,000 wealthy Van-
couverites who spent most of their time in Hawaii pretending
they're from Los Angeles while yammering about what a splen-
did place B.C is to visit and/or to exploit. Dwellers in LotusLand
have seen their numbers swelled by Hong Kong's financial
refugees in recent years, and it is now compulsory to spend at
least a week each year skiing at Whistler. But attitudes and behaviours in LotusLand are otherwise unaltered by a quarter century of self-delusion and environmental and economic abuse.
In the real world, Southwestern B.C. has rainy summers, sui-
cide-inducing winters and an obliviousness to the declining
Third World economy of the rest of British Columbia.

ATTILA LUKACS
Homo-erotic visual artist quickly going over the hill in mid-
European steam-baths and art galleries.

THE LUNATIC FRINGE
No, not B.C. and Alberta. These are born-yesterday political

movements who've made the Rhinoceros Party adherents seem like moderates who lack any sense of the ridiculous. One is the Heritage Front, Canada's only admitted racially motivated political party outside of the Parti Québécois. Most of the fringe parties are less nasty, but still harbour beliefs in things like Elvis, UFOs, Black, Asian and Jewish conspiracies, and other tenuous grips on reality. The Natural Law Party, a recent federal farce, believes that the road to good management lies through a national Yogic frequent flyer program. These believers are likely to become more extremist in their views as Reform and other elements of the mainstream parties stop pretending they're sane and occupy the natural territories of the conventional lunatic fringe.

MARNIE MCBEAN

Rower. More fun to watch than Silken Laumann for any number of reasons, not the least of which is her enigmatic grin. Evidently she knows something the rest of us haven't gotten onto....

MAC COSMETICS

Any company that uses k d lang and RuPaul to flog cosmetics has to be onto something — or be on something. If the company still exists in eighteen months and is still Canadian-owned, *then* it'll be a Canadian success story.

BRUCE MCDONALD

Movie director, road warrior. His lifelong project as a movie maker is to remake *Easy Rider* with 100 percent Canadian content, and he's talented enough to succeed.

DON MACDONALD

Former Federal Liberal cabinet minister and Canadian architect of the FTA. He is a member of the Trilateral Commission, if you're into conspiracy theories.

SIR JOHN A. MACDONALD

Political genius and whiskey enthusiast who invented Canada by giving alternate sections of land across the country to capitalists on the understanding that they would build a railroad and provide rail passenger service in perpetuity. The "perpetuity" ended in the mid-1980s without anyone in the government demanding the land back.

AUDREY MCLAUGHLIN

Former NDP national leader fond of making speeches that pointed out the obvious so ineffectively that only trade union leaders continued to find the obvious attractive and sufficiently obvious. Latest in a long line of proofs that "ordinary Canadians" so beloved of the NDP and its leadership are no more capable of running the country than the rich poufters we've been getting.

ALEXIS MCDONUT

She's sharper, more intelligent and funnier than 97 percent of male politicians, and she isn't boring when she's able to untangle the party line from around her neck. But she's probably going to end up as Audrey, Part II because her party is one long intellectual aneurysm.

RON MCLEAN

Sports journalist, straight man for Don Cherry on *Hockey Night in Canada*, amateur referee and maybe the nicest person in Canadian media. He has intelligence, civility and he can see outside and beyond the tunnel vision of sports. If Canada survives—and we're assuming that McLean can continue to survive working with Don Cherry—it will be because quietly intelligent people like Ron McLean help us to define ourselves as meaningfully not-American. His interview—or attempted interview—with Donovan Bailey after the Olympic 100 metres race in 1996 was an unintentional lesson in Canadian forbearance, and as revealing as (and infinitely more charming than) the blowhard American self-aggrandizement that ruined nearly everything else in the Olympics.

MACLEANS

Time/Newsweek poor cousin that demonstrates that average Canadians are even more stupid than average Americans, and that their writers can make even more crisply imbecilic summaries of national and world events than their American counterparts—and that cultural protections are sometimes wasted on the Canadian magazine industry.

SARAH MCLACHLAN

She's written some very good songs and she's young and gifted enough to get even better. But she's New Age, she's from Vancouver, and she's *way* too impressed by her own talent.

MARSHALL MCLUHAN

1960s communications speed-freak and corporate raconteur who was hounded by packs of wild academic and media dogs into total incomprehensibility. The grandfather of today's SuperMinds, McLuhan was primarily a gifted intellectual thief and an assembler of ideas. His weakness was his devout Roman Catholicism, which made him imagine that there was a Godly order within communications trends that subsequent events and developments have not revealed.

RITA MACNEIL

Unintentional CBC logo (more so now that she's defected to Baton Broadcasting) and an object lesson in what happens when the fat lady sings way too loud and far too often. It's mean to say things about someone with so many difficulties to live with, but geez, Merv Griffin has a better singing voice.

LINDA MCQUAIG

Generally reliable leftist journalist and always creative researcher—except when she's talking about the left or leftist alternatives to right wing proposals. Still she is arguably the only left of centre analyst who understands the monetary and banking systems.

CLAYTON MATCHEE

Non-commissioned Airborne officer accused of participating in the murder of Somalian teenager Shidane Arone. Machee isn't a nice man, but you don't have to worry that he'll show up at a dinner party. He's in a military hospital after a suicidal drug overdose, permanently camouflaged as a turnip, letting Kyle Brown, the only man below him in the incident's chain-of-command, take the rap for the killing. The only threat Machee now constitutes to the Canadian public is that his current state of consciousness makes him a prime candidate for the Senate. Those responsible for Arone's death, meanwhile, are free.

ERIC MALLING
W-5's television ideologue, and enthusiast for things New Zealandish. Malling was so right wing and brutish that CTV stuck a muzzle on him and on W-5.

ALBERTO MANGUEL
Often called "Ubiquito" in cultural circles, this Argentine-raised anthologist and critic, despite being a one-person multicultural group who speaks most of the nation's official and unofficial languages, was one of the first commentators to smell a rat in cultural equity policies. Manguel's good manners, appreciative reading habits, and the fact that he's almost always to be found on a continent other than North America gives outsiders the impression that Canada is a civilized country.

ELIZABETH MANLEY
Thrilled everyone in the country, herself most of all, by winning the 1988 Olympic Silver medal in women's singles and getting romantically involved with Doug Gilmour. She's been hanging around with Muppets, Smurfs, Care Bears and a wide variety of genderless Disney figurines of various species ever since. Needs new makeup consultant.

PRESTON MANNING

Bible-puncher, gay community pinup boy, speech-slick and son of former Alberta Social Credit Premier Ernest Manning. Preston became a culture hero for Canadian Old Age Pensioners, disaffected Chartered Accountants and other right-of-centre WASP remnants, mainly in Western Canada mostly by speaking slowly enough for them to understand. Manning's speech impediment makes him sound like he's talking through a mouthful of horse manure, which is something Alberta politics provides plenty of opportunity to practise. He did provide nearly all the moments of near-reality in the 1997 federal election but even with the contact lenses and the denim shirts, he's not a convincing cowboy.

MANITOBA

Flood zone and mosquito-breeding area, famous for being the geographic centre of Canada, at least within a twenty mile radius of Winnipeg city hall.

TORONTO MAPLE LEAFS

It isn't clear to anyone in Ontario whether this is Toronto's hockey team, a lucrative sports franchise, a valuable piece of real estate, or a fifty year experiment to determine how much damage autocratic management can do to a community amenity and national institution. Will Leafs president, Ken Dryden, who has been the most intelligent person in hockey since the 1970s, be able to clarify? Stay tuned.

MARIJUANA

There's now only eleven people left in the country who *really* believe marijuana use leads to heroin and cocaine addiction, and eight or nine more who think all that crap about it ruining short-term memory is real. Wow. Let's see, where was I? Oh yeah. Marijuana is the most logical pulp and paper crop for our forestry clearcuts once the trees are gone.

THE MARITIMES
Quaint set of territories similar to New England except with icebergs, odd accents and a more or less total absence of jobs and industries. Burial ground of choice for Canadian government industrial development programs since Halifax was blown up by stray armaments ship during the WW I. The only other exciting event to happen there was Leon Trotsky's short internment during the 1930s. High unemployment levels have recently resulted in UIC cards being taken for internal passports. Maritimers throw the best parties in Canada, which is *not* an admission that the poor have more fun.

MARKETING BOARDS
An administrative device created for a number of Canadian industries (mainly agricultural) to protect them from having their larger American counterparts dump products into the Canadian market below cost. The idea was to ensure a minimum level of Canadian production, and thus a degree of freedom from dependency on the United States. Sensible in their origins and basic purpose, marketing boards remind us that open and fair competition isn't a simple matter of lining up the horses and letting them run as fast as they can.

PAUL MARTIN, JR.

Michael Wilson with a red tie and a disingenuous grin. Doubles as Jean Chrétien's brain, which was supposed to be Lloyd Axworthy's job until it was discovered that Axworthy's brain could be disconnected from his spine with a simple downturn in fiscal spending priorities. Martin owns a steamship company that won't employ Canadian workers and doesn't pay Canadian taxes.

MARCEL MASSE

Mulroney-era cabinet minister, Québécois nationalist, and slight-of-hand artist who managed to transfer massive blocks of federal funds to a series of ludicrous and unnecessary projects in Quebec. He got away with it by vigorously denying what any dimwit could see he obviously was doing, and then swaddling himself in whichever flag (Canadian, Québécois or U.S.) was situationally appropriate. Jean Chrétien replaced him in the first post-Mulroney Federal Cabinet by a man named Marcel Masse.

ROBIN MATHEWS

Obscure B.C.-born U.S.-educated university professor who vociferously and accurately protested the American takeover and control of Canadian university faculties during the 1960s on up to, let's see, late last week. Unfortunately Mathews' most passionate policies are that a) all U.S.-born professors should be deported and replaced by Canadian-born industrial workers who have lost limbs in work-related mishaps, and b) foreign-born university professors should not be accorded the right to become loyal Canadian citizens like other people do. Example of a good idea whose time has come and gone—and alas, has turned into a lingering stink-bomb.

MAY 24th
Queen Victoria's birthday, whoever she was. Last day for the suicidal to try skidooing on Canadian lakes.

JOHN BENTLEY MAYS
Chronically depressed American dilettante who, despite never having met anyone who actually lived in a surburb, has gradually honed his observational skills to the point that his occasional newspaper columns on Toronto's architecture and urban design have become a unique cultural event—unless he's extolling Modernism or the private pleasures of the outer colonies of Toronto.

m b a n x
Bank of Montreal with Bob Dylan's help, plus heaps of the so/so. Sure, a bank could make a difference. It could even change. But it would have to want to, right? And it would have to be more profitable than before. Now give up the dumb questions and wake up!

MEECH LAKE
Bloodsucker-loaded recreational lake in the Gatineau Hills east of Ottawa that inspired Brian Mulroney's first organized attempt to dismantle Canada. The Meech Lake deal, which was agreed to by nine drugged or drunk premiers, was foiled only because a Native Indian MPP from Manitoba objected and the premier of

Newfoundland woke up at the last minute. Birthplace of the political oxymoron "distinct society".

WENDY MESLEY

CBC's cleverest journalist, which she once proved by outwitting the entire herd of male TVheads at CBC in a game-show format test of current events presided over by Peter Mansbridge. Mansbridge reacted to her clearly superior grasp of the official facts by refusing to let her answer further questions, allowing David Halton to win. Not long after that, Mesley married Mansbridge, thus contextualizing the common sense of CBC journalists. Yet despite her personal life, she remains among the very few news-reading blocks of wood in Canadian television who gives a convincing impersonation of someone who understands what he/she's reading off the teleprompters.

METIS

Western Canadian term for Mohawks: a little Native blood, a lot of attitude and the same lust for casinos and cross-border trade that characterizes official Indians.

METROTOWN, BURNABY, B.C.

Plague Mall #2: The set of *Bladerunner* with your crazy uncle Mort's electric train set running through the middle of it. Features Canada's most lethal underground parking maze outside of Toronto's City Hall.

MEXICO

We got into bed with this country in 1993 by signing NAFTA and being told that sending our industries southward to be attended by workers forced to labour without security, safety or a livable minimum wage would somehow help us and raise the Mexican worker's quality of life. Mexico's monetary system quickly collapsed, its soldiers began shooting its citizens, the president who negotiated NAFTA turned out to be a gangster and the already disgusting gulf between its rich and poor grew wider. But it was all inevitable, right? Part of progress and evolution. A natural partner.

MIRABEL AIRPORT

Federal line department fuckup *extraordinaire* from the late 1960s. The federal government expropriated 95,000 acres of Quebec farmland for this never-used white elephant, pushing Québécois families from farms they'd worked since the 17th Century, providing convincing evidence that Canada is too insensitive an instrument to govern Quebec.

ED MIRVISH

Toronto businessman and public vulgarian who has put his money wherever his mouth and ego have uncovered public value. You can question Mirvish's taste if you want, but not his commitment or his generosity. If Canada had a hundred people like him, this would be a truly entertaining and maybe great country. It wouldn't have good restaurants or an indigenous theatre community, but it would be cheap to live in, the poor would get enough to eat and it would be more fun than the one we've got.

JONI MITCHELL

Saskatchewan folksinger who lost her grasp of major keys in the 1980s but remains one of Canada's few decent poets and among the few Canadian entertainers who never loses her dignity or violates her own privacy for commercial purposes. Perhaps the best measure of Mitchell's personal dignity is the way she was able to publicize the existence of a daughter given up for adoption thirty years ago, find the daughter and integrate her into her life without it being turned into a nightmare of soap opera sentimentalities.

MONETARY SYSTEM

Until the early 1980s Canada enjoyed a relatively independent monetary system, along with a highly centralized and secure banking system and a high level of local investment and moderately high personal savings. In less than fifteen years American-style deregulation, foreign takeovers and chicken-shit government policies have made us a capital and profit flight zone with a dependent and volatile currency, preyed on by a criminally profitable banking sector wholly divorced from responsibility to local and national well-being.

MONOPOLIES

Twenty years ago both Canada and the U.S. had strong legislation to safeguard citizens against the formation of unfair monopolies that would reduce the competition which is supposedly the source of capitalism's vitality. A very large portion of Canada's anti-combines energy went into worrying about the effects increasing multinational corporate agglomeration could have on the country's fragile cultural integrity. But at almost exactly the point in our history where the policies and programs for culture were producing decent cultural products and one or two artists able to compare with the world's best, a cloud of flies lands in the ointment. The cycle of radical agglomeration and mergers, along with the open conspiracy no legislator can acknowledge but which is reducing competition, standardizing markets, and applying a cybernetic choke-hold on the flow of dissident views began to gain ascendancy.

One man now owns 58 percent of Canadian newspapers, while the ownership patterns in every other sector of the media and communications industries are falling into the hands of a shrinking circle of megawealthy individuals, families or syndicates. Arguably more dangerous to indigenous culture is that the media, like every other sector of the overall economy is being transformed into machine parts within multinational combines wholly divorced from any human concern other than that of ensuring shareholder profits.

MONTREAL

This once great city is being reduced to hostile enclaves by xenophobes on both sides of Lucien Bouchard's frontal lobes. Yet it is still a remarkable city. There are those innumerable casual moments where Montrealers will shift from English to French in the middle of sentences without finding it unusual, there is the ironwork staircases, the grandiose modernist architecture, the charm of the cathedrals and the scent — not quite of Paris but of a cosmopolitanism — unlike anything anywhere. It makes you wistful about how great this country might have been. Particularly when you realize there is a possibility that

Montreal could end up to Canada what Berlin was to Germany
during the Cold War.

MICHAEL MOORE
Creator of documentary film *Roger and Me*, and Canada's ill-
kempt White Hope south of the border.

FRANK MOORES
Former Newfoundland premier and lobbyist alleged to have
been willing to lobby for the highest bidder willing to open secret Swiss bank accounts for his employers.

HENRY MORGENTALER
Abortion pro-choice culture hero undeterred by death threats
and exploding clinics. He motors on, unsmiling, unrelentingly
logical in his commitment to women's choice. Now that we live
in a country where the governing powers don't even pretend to
care about the nation's children, why does this stupid debate
over whether or not women should bring more unwanted children into the world continue? To distract us from the real problem we face?

ALANIS MORISSETTE
Alright. So she talked about giving head in a rock and roll song.
Someone take their foot off the cat's tail before we all go mad.

MOTION PICTURE INDUSTRY
A euphemism for U.S.-based Japanese-owned open conspiracy
to prevent people from seeing accurate depictions of their lives.

The Motion Picture Industry builds movies to formulas too tight for creativity, spends astronomical amounts of money on special effects that addict the weak-minded and prevent poorer outsiders from competing with movies about human beings.

FARLEY MOWAT

Writer and *bon vivant* who devolved into a children's writer— possibly under the strain of serious research. During the height of the Cold War in the 1960s he was permitted inside Russia, but merely asked where the best bars were. The credibility of his research has been questioned by *Saturday Night* magazine, which may or may not be worrisome in light of that magazine's willingness to excerpt anything written by Elspeth Cameron, including her recent half-cooked lesbian revelations, as gospel truth. Even if Mowat spent only thirty minutes dancing with wolves and living with aboriginals, *Never Cry Wolf*, and *People of the Deer* are perfectly readable books for young adults almost a half-century after they were written.

BRIAN MULRONEY

Canadian prime minister 1984-92 who carries the distinction of having a smaller percentage of voters support his government than the segment of the population who believes that Elvis is still alive. Has a lifelong fetish about singing Irish folk songs while sitting on the knees of American corporate captains. Any other country in the world would have impeached, assassinated or splattered him with noxious-smelling substances after his first two years in office. Canadians reelected him. Whether or not Mulroney had Swiss bank accounts, as the RCMP alleged, doesn't matter. Why he was allowed to spend eight years shoveling our national assets across negotiating tables to anyone willing to grab them, does.

MULTICULTURALISM

Originally an offshoot of unofficial federal government programs to ensure that Canada's drive-in restaurants would have enough dishwashers, multiculturalism eventually devolved into a two-pronged immigration strategy aimed at securing workers willing to labour at minimum wage jobs and for securing offshore investment capital. The strategy didn't include telling incoming immigrants (capital-intensive or otherwise) that Canada had customs, laws and a culture they ought to learn, a climate they're not supposed to whine about, and that Canadian citizenship involves duties more extensive than working long enough hours to buy a Camaro.

Multiculturalism is rare outside the major cities and is in the process of being exterminated within Quebec. Elsewhere in the country it is practised on a smaller scale under the disguise of common sense and basic decency—provided that new participants can afford the $900 entry fee. In the prairie provinces immigration remains restricted to countries where people like to folk dance in colourful costumes and have a genetic interest in heavy machinery.

In spite of government intentions, multiculturalism has evolved into a phenomenon that, due to the tenacity, imagination and aggression of its intended exploitees is rapidly replacing Canada's dowdy Euro-WASP cultural fabric with a slightly shredded but more colourful and vibrant weave.

Criticizing multiculturalism is a little like shooting fish in a barrel, but everyone should remember this before firing: if Canada doesn't self-destruct as a nation state before the globalist/New Conservative revolution burns itself out, the experiment of large-scale immigration into a hybrid-nation with a weak national identity will be one of the crucial political experiments of the 21st Century.

ALICE MUNRO

Famous writer of tiny, perfect stories about the bitterness of incapacity, the richness of WASP stoicisms and other subjects suitable for conversation at a quilting bee. Had she chosen another trade, she'd have been a jeweller who crafted exquisitely complex brooches for elderly women. Some folks think she needs to hang out with more interesting people.

MURKANS

A species of Americans who are the ones Canadians ought to be worrying about. Murkans own massive quantities of household automatic weapons and model themselves politically and intellectually on Richard Nixon and G. Gordon Liddy. Today, Newt Gingrich, Christine Whitman, Pat Buchanan and about 100,000 large, repressed and angry males of various backgrounds hanging out around bars and taverns across the U.S. are the primary Murkan threats to Canada. Unlike Americans, who are perpetually wet behind the ears when it comes to the *realpolitik*, Murkans understand the nuances of invasion tactics and the infinitely repeatable ways in which invasion, blockade and subversion can be masked as international trade equalization, capitalist progress and other incontrovertible inevitabilities of the 1990s.

REX MURPHY

CBC Mediafave. Judging from his permanent grimace and delivery style, he's there to represent that small but vocal minority of Canadians with screwdrivers stuck in sensitive zones of the body.

ANNE MURRAY

Nova Scotia physical education instructor and erotomania target who sings alto and dances the on-stage foxtrot like your Uncle Moe. She's a small price to pay for the CRTC's CanCon regulations and to keep the elderly happy and entertained, but please, please, no more television specials.

MAGIC MUSHROOMS

Chief item in B.C.'s underground economy and the only major industry willing to employ workers under twenty-five. The tiny psychedelics are said to grow so well between the runways at Vancouver International that small planes occasionally crash land there merely to get at them.

MUSIC INDUSTRY

Canadians garnered thirty Grammy nominations in 1996, and things are supposed to be getting better. But we still only produce 15 percent of the music we hear, and in the wee hours of the morning, are we really safe with the sounds of David Foster, Celine Dion, Bryan Adams, Rush, and Alanis Morissette filling our ears?

ZEBRA MUSSELS

A tiny freshwater mollusk introduced to the Great Lakes by the KGB at the height of the Cold War. The little suckers clog up water intakes and foul boat hulls, but they've also done more to clean up Lake Erie than the combined efforts of Canada and the U.S. We should put zebra mussels on the back of the forthcoming five dollar coin to celebrate one species that won't be extinct in the near future, and to recognize the way things *really* get done in this country. A federal program to import herds of African zebras to the Great Lakes as a biological control was said to have been under active consideration at Environment Canada before the agency was disbanded.

ALANA MYLES

How many truckloads of whiskey did it take to create that voice and face? And how many people understand the lyrics to *Black Velvet*?

NAFTA

1992 agreement between U.S., Canada and Mexico aimed at funnelling jobs to Mexico, profits to U.S. multinational centres and distracting Canadians with empty New Conservative slogans about becoming more competitive while the country's assets are trucked south by American trucking companies using Mexican drivers.

NAPO

National AntiPoverty Organization. It is nearly as predictable as its contrary BCNI, and certain to diametrically opposite views.

Somewhere near the midpoint between these two lobbies is where you'll discover what the issues really are.

NATIONALISM

Canada's nationalism is unique in the world. It is not xenophobic and does not require citizens to wave flags, get drunk at high-school and college football games, place hands over hearts, start wars, or engage in other jingoistic behaviours. Canadian nationalism has an exquisitely noble purpose: to keep Canadians from becoming citizens of the United States.

NATIVE SELF-DETERMINATION

Determination of native leaders in Canada to be able to sit on and oversee the activities of all government bodies and corporate boards of directors in Canada and to make long, boring speeches about animals and spirits without being asked to lighten up and get real.

NATIVE SELF-GOVERNMENT

Euphemism adopted by Canadian governments to tag the practice of allowing Pre-European immigrants to determine what they would like to be and do provided that it doesn't impinge on corporate resource harvesting and any other high-priority financial sector pastimes.

NCC

National Citizens' Coalition. This occasionally funny gang of aggrieved white guys was started by David Smith, headed by David Somerville and now run as a many-headed dog that will bark at anything to the left of extreme libertarianism. It is the highly organized property-rights lunatic fringe of the Reform Party, which sounds like a redundancy but isn't.

NDP

New Democratic Party: formerly social democrats with strong ideas about social justice they occasionally embarrassed Liberals and Conservatives into implementing. Currently a coalition of

a) neophyte capitalists willing to delude themselves that dogs don't eat dogs;

b) Safety Nazis bent on strapping all free-standing objects or persons to walls and floors; and

c) Trade Unionists who will sacrifice any democratic institution or industry to protect the union privileges of anyone over forty-five.

NEOCONS

Disgruntled Liberal and NDP party members, not to be confused with New Conservatives or Conservative Intellectuals, who loathe Neocons the way Norwegians loathe Mr. Quisling. There are a lot of NeoCons, and they tend to play a lot of golf and vote for the Reform party.

NEP/NEB

Trudeau-era national energy policy instrument (not to be confused with 1930s Soviet New Economic Plans) that crashed shortly after takeoff, leaving behind the massively debt-ridden PetroCan, Alberta's tar sands project and the still-born Newfoundland Offshore Oil project. The former two have been sold off, debt free, to the corporate sector, but a small pipeline from Ottawa intermittently pours dollars into the holds of multinational money tankers anchored off the Newfoundland coast to keep both projects on the books.

NEVER TRUST ANYONE WHO GRINS WHILE THEY SPEAK
Paul Martin, Jr., Preston Manning, Ralph Klein, Hana Gartner, Brian Mulroney

NEW CONSERVATIVES
The ideologically involved right wing of the conservative movement. They tend to be young business dorks of both genders, and they're our own special chapter of the international movement that believes employed workers are the chief impediment to wealth, and that the poor should be kicked hard in order to make the rich wealthier. David Frum is a leading New Conservative.

NEWFOUNDLAND
Nature park for chronic unemployment, folksinging and icebergs that gave up its autonomy and its fish in 1949 for the promise that Canada would find a publisher for Joey Smallwood's books, provide dental care and climate improvement, and maybe transfer a few viable industries from Ontario. The Federal government dental hygiene programs have been almost as ineffective as the Navy has been in defending the fishery: unemployment levels threaten to reach 75 percent, the fishery is closed, the only industry brought in involved imaginary oil rigs that drowned as many Newfoundland workers as they employed.

The icebergs are now being studied along with island's over-supply of comedians as a source of potential new exports, while the remaining Newfoundlanders go around threatening to start clubbing seals again, along with a few people in Ottawa and Quebec they suspect are responsible for destroying the fishery, stealing hydro resources and otherwise screwing up things.

PETER C. NEWMAN

Czech-born Hudson's Bay salesperson and author of popular histories that don't sell very well. This Upper Canada College grad is Canada's most convincing political gossip, for which, according to a bunch of over-sixty journalists who are also UCC grads, we're supposed to be grateful.

NEWSPAPERS

Canada's most suicidal media/communications subsector. Corporate agglomeration has reduced the total number of papers operating by close to 50 percent in the last two decades, and editorial and local coverage by 90 percent. If all newspapers want to do is list sports scores and stock market results, publish photos of newly appointed business executives and pull entertainment industry PR releases off the wire services, how long will it be before all of Canada's newspapers originate from a single office in Toronto staffed by fifteen or twenty digital technicians who all look vaguely like Andrew Coyne and are salaried by Conrad Black?

NEW YEAR'S

Once an evening and following day when the Scots got dead drunk and complained gloomily about the English, it has been taken over by celebration culture maniacs and RIDE roadblocks to ensure that future generations don't have any fun either. See *festival culture*

NEW YORK CITY

Where Torontonians phone to find out how they're supposed to behave in complex situations. Quebec residents would like to do the same, but can't understand the behaviour codings due to the language barrier. Because New York solves problems by hiring more police, it has become the New Conservative's urban redevelopment model for major Canadian cities.

NIAGARA FALLS

Zone of extreme commercial vulgarity overlaid on one of The Seven Wonders of the World. If you want a perfect example of the aesthetic collision between early 20th Century public trust and late 20th Century mercantile "trust nothing", go to Niagara Falls. The falls have the world's longest active tenure as a disposal unit for depressives, exhibitionists and fools. And oh yeah. *Our* falls are grander and prettier than *theirs*.

NON-LIARS

Margaret Atwood, Ted Byfield, Dalton Camp, Don Cherry, Michael Valpy, Mary Walsh

THE NORTH

A vague area thought by Torontonians to be somewhere north of Barrie and Lake Muskoka suitable for Native land claims, hydroelectric megaprojects and sanitary landfills. For most other

Canadians the North is one of three things:

a) something you brag about when you're drunk and American tourists are annoying you;

b) a place to avoid; or

c) a vast area north of the 60th parallel populated during the winter by Native Indians and Inuit, some extremely picturesque but mostly bad-tempered wild animals, ice, air pollution levels equivalent to those in Los Angeles, and no ozone in the upper atmosphere. During the summer, one can expect to find an additional 40 billion blackflies, and a slightly smaller number of nature photographers.

NOTWITHSTANDING

The linguistic rat in the granary of the cultural exemption Canada gained with the Canada U.S. Free Trade Agreement in 1988 and with NAFTA in 1993. The "notwithstanding" clause tacked onto the exemption allows U.S. traders the right of retaliation—to equivalent commercial value—to any attempt the Canadian government makes to protect Canadian cultural institutions. Thus, no serious new protections have been attempted since 1988, and those that were already in the works were met with a hail of American threats, and thus died quietly on order papers and in Ottawa back rooms. Wary Canadians duck whenever they hear this word spoken by anyone in a position of authority.

NUKES

Canada's Atomic Energy Commission specializes in the design, development and sale of obsolete nuclear reactors to such politically stable areas as Iraq, Pakistan, Rumania and Ontario. For decades, Northern Ontario was the source of much of the world's raw uranium, which is only one of the factors that makes it a leading candidate to become the eventual repository for the world's supply of spent uranium and other nuclear wastes and byproducts. This will obviate the need for street lighting in northern communities or the settling of land claims with Northern Ontario's Native Indians.

OBSCENITY

Thanks to a unique convergence of Christian traditionalism and full-fanged feminism in, of all places, the chambers of the Supreme Court of Canada, you can now commit the crime of obscenity any time you make a sexual image (in words or pictures) that someone decides to find offensive. The Supreme Court's R. v Butler judgement of 1992 redefined legal "harm" (previously thought to require, minimally, that you punch someone) to include the "perception" of harm, "especially to women" in the representations of sex. The harm, wrote Justice John Sopinka, in a unanimous decision, consists of people, especially guys, acquiring bad attitudes that *might* lead them to do bad things. The judgement has made our highest court an intellectual laughing-stock in law journals across the English-speaking world.

OBERON PRESS

Ottawa-based small press dedicated to collecting government grants and printing "works of literature" in badly designed formats and unreadable typefaces and then making no serious attempt to market them. Anyone willing to autopsy the history and behaviour of this archetypal instrument of Canadian public cultural subsidy will understand why Canada is losing its ability to defend its artistic culture.

OCTOBER 17, 1970

For some it marks the Canadian equivalent of U.S. Kent State massacre perpetrated by then-Prime Minister Pierre Elliott Trudeau in response to "perceived threat" of a Quebec insurrection by a group of separatists who'd been smoking too much dope. It involved the prime minister acting tough on television, police and military personnel running loose for a couple of weeks arresting and generally being impolite to several hundred members of the middle class who displayed attitude problems. The arrests gave Quebec dissidents the impetus to start a serious separatist movement under René Lévesque, and gave English Canadian intellectuals the moral élan to go out and protest against the Vietnam War like good Americans.

OFDC

Ontario Film Development Corporation: wildly successful Ontario provincial government adjunct to Telefilm Canada that helped to foster a small but vigorous feature film and documentary industry in Ontario. It was killed for its successes, which Ontario's Harris Government decided were communistic.

OFFSHORE LENDERS

According to the federal government, these are salt-of-the-earth philanthropists generous enough to hold Canada's public debt for us. In many cases, these people got their investment capital inside Canada by buying majority stakes in Canadian industries, sucking them dry for profits, and then reinvesting the money in extremely generous government bond issues.

OIL
Political substance that, if mixed with bourbon or rye whiskey, propels consumers to the far right of the political spectrum. Canada has sufficient oil and gas reserves to turn Alberta's economy into a small-scale facsimile of Mexico's.

OKA
Costume party, real-estate brawl, media event that backfired on everyone involved except for owners of military surplus clothing stores.

THE OKANAGAN VALLEY
Formerly one of Canada's prime fruit-growing areas, famous for its good weather, Social Credit premiers and the Ogopogo, which is a tourism industry invention from the 1950s that about four people in the valley still believe in. The Okanagan is rapidly filling to capacity with trailer parks for the elderly, and it is a prime terminus point for mall and sunshine-loving questers from all over Western Canada, who believe they've discovered Arizona.

CLIFFORD OLSON
He has no place in this dictionary. Neither has Ernst Zundel. In certain cases silence is the most articulate and effective critique.

MICHAEL ONDAATJE

Shy, gracious and intelligent poet who has become an international celebrity with the transformation of his Booker Prize-winning novel *The English Patient* into an Academy Award winning motion picture. Ondaatje's only response to fame has been to become even more shy and gracious, and to gain twenty pounds so the starlets won't hit on him. Twenty-five years from now, he'll still be famous, but for writing a book titled *Coming Through Slaughter*, which radically widened the boundaries by which young Canadian writers were able to approach their craft.

ONTARIO

Canada's largest and most confused province has at least four distinct regions:

a) Metro Toronto, which would rather be New York City only cleaner and safer;

b) Southwestern Ontario, which just wants the Auto Pact to live on so everyone can afford to stay drunk on American beer;

c) Eastern Ontario, where it borders Lake Ontario, which is obsessed with breeding hockey players and ridiculing Quebec-bred hockey players as contact-shy wimps;

d) The northern regions of Ontario, which are distinguished by ridiculously long winters, prehistoric rocks, mercury poisoning, and several glow-in-the dark mining communities which are the result of excessive anti-Communist zeal at the Atomic Energy Commission of Canada a few decades ago.

ORCHESTRAS AND OPERAS

Following the tradition of 18th and 19th century European centres, nearly every Canadian city larger than North Battleford,
Saskatchewan, has or is planning to have both a symphony
orchestra and an opera company. All are heavily subsidized by
both government and the corporate sector, and cater almost
exclusively to the tastes of wealthy urbanites, who don't appear
to have noticed that the 20th Century has yet to produce any
orchestral music comparable to that of the 18th. Nor have they
noticed that opera has been replaced as a culturally significant
activity, first by Hollywood and Broadway musicals, then by
television soap operas, and recently by Rita MacNeil. On the
other hand, why not have a regular excuse to wear tuxedos and
other formal garb?

ORDINARY WORKING CANADIANS

Citizens the NDP believe will faithfully vote for them in elections. 20-30 percent of low income Canadian workers do—
when they have the energy to vote at all.

OTTAWA

Mosquito and snow-befouled city located on a defunct canal
system thought to lead in the direction of Washington, D.C. In
the 1960s and 1970s Ottawa was the Brazilia of the northern
hemisphere, but now more resembles Rio. Current population
mainly taken up by poultry breeding schemes aimed at perfect-
ing an all-white-meat chicken, and furious paper-shuffling.
Current federal government plans are aimed at turning Ottawa
into a ghost town by 2005.

OWNER/OPERATORS

Alan Greenspan

Chairman, U.S. Federal Reserve Board. He's the guy who tells the Bank of Canada how to experiment on us next.

BCNI

Business Council on National Issues. Most powerful corporate lobby in Canada. Michael Wilson sat on its knee and clacked his jaw. Paul Martin, Jr. is now on the perch.

Moody's Investor Service

Bond rater. When these guys call Canadian governments in for a conference, there is fear and trembling.

Margaret Thatcher

She's been out of office in Britain for over a decade, but she's now running Canada and the U.S. in spirit along with Milton Freedman, and threatening to take over Europe.

OZONE LAYER

What Canada has progressively less of each year. Instead of vigorous programs to find alternatives to freon gas and protect and enhance atmospheric ozone levels, Canadian governments whine about the problem in harmony with the U.S. government agencies, and set loose a well-funded agency to inform citizens about how dangerous it is to their health to be outdoors without a body-suit, a hat, gloves, a parasol, and #45 sunblock.

VAUGHN PALMER

Aggrieved White Guy, veteran *Vancouver Sun* small-c conservative provincial pundit with the temperament of an overfed por-
cupine. Prickly about infinite government malfeasance, but
lazily uninterested in social policy, culture, environment, and
subjects beyond the reach of his sharp quills. Has written about
750 columns in a row attacking B.C. NDP governments, which
have been in office since 1991. Major West Coast contributor to
the media's demonization of public sphere.

JACQUES PARIZEAU

Recent Quebec separatist leader, premier and poutine-
enhanced Lee Van Cleef look-alike. Parizeau led Quebec's 1995
attempt to escape from Canada until Lucien Bouchard took
over. Resigned as premier after pointing out that if everybody in
Quebec were French-speaking and of French origin, Quebec
could be a republic with racial and cultural policies that were
just as much fun as the ones in Serbia, Croatia and Slovenia.
Parizeau is currently drinking 7-Up, pondering imponderables,
studying the career of Cardinal Richelieu and jamming his foot
into his mouth whenever Bouchard needs someone to take a fall
for him or the media are stuck for a story.

PARLIAMENT

Before recent leaders decided to Americanize the Canadian political system, parliament was the governing legislative body of
Canada. Members now alternately comatose and hysterical
while they await their pensions and the results of cabinet ses-

sions. The advent of parliamentary television has led to an illicit trade in amphetamines and other awakeness-simulating drugs.

PARTNERSHIPS
Recently invented cultural procedure in which governments and corporations leap into bed, pretend to hump one another, then invite the public to sit on the end of the bed for the announcement that, in the interests of economic growth and sound management, tax burdens have been shifted from the corporations to the general public, and that cultural programs will henceforth be funded by the corporate sector.

PEACEKEEPERS
Troops sent to political hot-zones to keep crazed ethnic groups from murdering one another, and to keep enough of our armed forces outside the country so that we'll remember we're not Americans. Canada's most successful peacekeeping foray has been in Cyprus, where Canadians and others have kept Greek and Turkish factions from their genocidal destinies for three decades. Canadian peacekeepers in Cambodia, Bosnia and Somalia have been—how can this be put delicately—notably less successful in recent years.

LESTER B. PEARSON
Nobel prize-winning Canadian diplomat, he was a sleep-inducing prime minister (1963-68) fond of being pissed on by American diplomats. He led Canada into a ludicrous debate over the design and colour of its flag during a period when the U.S. was

dismantling our foreign and military policy. On the other side, he was enough of a baseball fan to have almost single-handedly obtained Montreal a Major League baseball franchise for Expo 67. The fact that the CIA believed Pearson was a Communist probably led him to annoint Pierre Trudeau as his successor, thus giving us the only prime minister in the 20th Century who had real social democratic ideas and an IQ above the national average.

MATTHEW PERRY

Star of the television show *Friends*, but also the son of Pierre Trudeau's travelling companion/secretary Susan Perry. It's unclear if the association with Trudeau has elevated the younger Perry in any way—or if he recognizes who Trudeau was.

STAN PERSKY

One of the four or five most competent public intellectuals in the country, Persky is gay, leftist, American-born, oblivious to fashions of any sort, unfailingly, patiently, reasonable in his citizenly project to listen to everything and to insist that *nobody* has a right not to—and, so you know, one of my oldest and best friends. His book *Buddy's: Meditations on Desire* is one of a series of books he's written that investigate the reasons of the human heart.

ROSS PETTY

Hoofer, chaperone, cultural hangabout. One assumes he's related to someone with power. Perrin Beatty? Al Waxman? Currently masterminding an attempt to turn *The Nutcracker Suite* into a murder mystery series for television, or something equally bizarre but uninteresting.

MARLENE-NOURBESE PHILIPS

Public intellectual, anti-racism activist, grant recipient. Perhaps because her legal training makes her quick to litigate, it is sometimes hard to see that Phillips is among the most articulate members of a generation of leftist intellectuals who believe that democracy means having the right to be offended by anything with which one is not in exact agreement. Not surprisingly, the New Conservatives are rapidly appropriating the right to be offended, along with the quick litigation strategy.

POETS

Canada has more published poets per capita than any country in the world, which isn't surprising given that Canadian poetry as practised is overwhelmingly writing for people who don't want to think anything through. Since poetry is a commercially obsolete medium of expression, one could interpret this unabated statistic as a signal that Canada's publicly funded cultural system has failed to respond to common sense. Canada's successful poets usually play guitars and other musical instruments, and they're so easy to find I won't name them. I'll offer two poets, relatively unknown outside their communities, who give in to no vulgarities and write as clearly as the age allows: George Stanley, Anne Carson. Find them, read them.

POLITICAL PARTIES

If only they *would* party a little. Canadian political parties are too obsessed with raiding one another's ideological and demographic ground to have either fun or substantial ideas about the future they're selling down the river. Canada's Liberal party is no longer liberal, its social democratic party isn't social or democratic, and its conservatives control the country even though they have the fewest seats in Parliament of any recognized party. Just over a third of parliamentary seats are held by radically deranged representatives from our two main lunatic asylums, Quebec and Western Canada.

CANADIAN POLITICS

Politics in Canada used to mean whining about the government, but since GATT, deregulation and the various corporate-inspired free trade mechanisms have dismantled most of the means of controlling our political and economic structures, Canada doesn't really have politics, just a lot of politicians explaining why we can't do anything except cut programs while platoons of wild-eyed economists and bond raters run around telling the people we elected what to do.

The only policies any government in Canada has been serious about in the 1990s are those aimed at making it impossible for citizens to smoke a cigarette without being hounded and harassed by health professionals and other self-righteous nincompoops. It's not clear what we'll have to whine about after we've been reduced to a country of stateless non-smokers.

POLITICAL SYSTEM

Canada's devolving political system was once a British-style parliamentary system (albeit without the kinky, wig-wearing Lords and Ladies). It is now moving toward a nasty *mélange* of corporate boards of directors, U.S.-style rule-by-lobbies, and a lie-in-the-sun-crawl-under-the-nearest-rock expert systems modelled after the behaviour of desert reptiles. Canada's governments are currently supervised by U.S. bond-rating agencies, who are considering assuming direct management to guarantee investor confidence. See *investor confidence*

POSTAL UNIONS
Labour relations laboratory in which the corporate sector has been experimenting with union-breaking devices for two decades. The result has been the virtual collapse of the Canadian postal system.

POUTINE
French fries, CheezWhiz and chemical gravy. This piece of authentic Quebec cuisine is the best argument going for kicking Quebec out of Canada.

THE PRAIRIES
A permanently depressed economic region noted for its cultural vitality, derelict wheat fields, radical shifts in government, and a willingness to get drunk and forget about how flat it all is.

CHRISTOPHER PRATT
Hyperrealist painter who manages to be non-figurative at the same time. The artistic equivalent of Otrivin. Related to fellow-painter Mary Pratt, who also causes dry sinuses.

PREMIERS, PRIME MINISTERS AND FIRST MINISTERS

During periods of sanity, elected provincial leaders call themselves *Premiers*, leaving the *Prime Minister* designation to the elected Federal leader. In recent years, however, depending on the degree of provincial egomania and hostility, some *Premiers* have taken to annoying Ottawa by designating themselves *Prime Ministers*. Ottawa responds by dragooning all the *Premiers* to Ottawa for time-wasting protocol festivals and transfer payment cutback announcements. During these conferences everyone carefully uses the term *First Ministers*, although during planning sessions the *Premiers* and *Prime Minister* refer to one another as *Those Assholes,* which is closer to the way voters regard them while they're playing these silly games.

PRINCE EDWARD ISLAND

Former island province, now merely a potato patch and on-location site for Anne of Green Gables, Canada's primary cultural export. PEI's campaign to have everyone in the province declared an MP or senator has met with partial success only because the young, female Japanese tourists that constitute 40 percent of the island population during the summer don't yet qualify as citizens.

PUBLISHING INDUSTRY

Canada's publishing industry, nurtured over two decades to relative financial competence by modest government subsidies despite the inherent economy-of-scale disadvantages it must deal with, is now being asked to suck hard on the tailpipe of GATT and other globalization apparatuses that are expressly designed to supplant indigenous cultural instruments like, say, the Canadian publishing industry. Now, we all know that house cats don't turn into tigers, but one of the essential tests to see whether Canada deserves to go on being a real country will be the testing of the courage of Canada's publishers to see whether they'll be able to fight off the subsidy cuts and the economic levelling by our globalization-crazed governments and survive.

QUEBEC
Quebec's distinctive identity centres around the French language, even though Parisians dispute that French is actually spoken in Quebec. Other regional habits are separatism, referring to English Canadians as "exploiters" or "swine", and not showing up for constitutional and resource sales conventions organized by the Federal government to appease them. Québécois enjoy tearing down English-language signs, using real estate under Native land claims for golf courses and hydroelectric sites and eating caramelized maple sap laced with sulfuric acid straight off the snow.

QUEBEC CITY
Attempted tourism Mecca and Quebec capital. Quebec government is so addled by *Je me souviens* madness that it is selling off the Plains of Abraham for condominium development. Letting the Quebec Nordiques go to Colorado was Jacques Parizeau's way of biting off his nose to spite his face.

BLOC QUEBECOIS

Latest and best organized gang of joual-mumbling Federal Parliamentary blockheads dedicated to goading the governing party in Ottawa into tossing Quebec out of the confederation.

PARTI QUEBECOIS

Formerly a social democratic political party in Quebec led by René Lévesque and aimed at reenacting the Plains of Abraham battle of 1759 where British General Wolfe defeated a gang of drunken French soldiers under Montcalm. The party has gradually been taken over by crazed ethnocrats, language-deluded New Conservatives, church/state integrationists and Lucien Bouchard-for King enthusiasts. Separation referendums in 1980 and 1995 were inconclusive, except to let Quebec know that the financial community wasn't going to stand for much more nonsense from either side.

THE "QUEBEC QUESTION"

It is almost impossible to say anything about the Quebec Question that doesn't dissolve into instant cant, thanks to rednecks, sentimentalists, and a lot of truly mean-spirited people on both sides of the issue. Maybe the main point of the Quebec Question is that there *is* a serious question to be answered. It isn't enough to simply ask *"What does Quebec want?"* and then tie, bind and gag the question with sloppy metaphors about marriage, divorce, sex and raising children. The true question reads more like *"What would be a reasonable political arrangement for a hybrid-state historically shaped by trees, rivers, snow, and by francophone, anglophone and aboriginal immigrants, resulting in a diffuse national identity that has subsequently been diffused further by substantial further waves of human immigration from environments and cultures radically different from those that founded it?"*

Probably more important than asking ourselves stupidly obtuse questions is that we stop looking for simple answers to the questions under our noses. There aren't any simple answers. Other countries have figured out how to live with autonomous regions, self-governing peoples and even patchwork solutions that are far sillier than anything we're proposing. But almost anything would be an improvement on the present trajectory of the country, which seems intent on an absolute devolution of Confederation into a loose association of shopping megamalls.

QUEEN ELIZABETH II

Titular head of Canadian state and world's only sensible reigning monarch. Elizabeth's considerable political and diplomatic skills, notwithstanding her evident lack of any parenting ability, should make her the common sense choice to rule the country after the self-overthrow of the federal government is complete.

RACE RELATIONS

Notwithstanding all the good intentions, this is the most heavily policed social zone in Canadian history in which race and class relations are invariably conflated and confused, every ethnicity is permitted to be racist and common sense is thoroughly disabled. George Orwell would have been amused. . . .

BOB RAE

Former Ontario premier, and with Pierre Trudeau, one of the

only fully literate Canadians ever elected as a head of state. Rae couldn't handle his party's powerful Labour Brigade nor Ontario's corporate captains, and self-destructed three months into his government's term of office by falling into the hands of his party's safety Nazis, who were the only people left in Ontario willing to support him. Now a *Toronto Star* book reviewer and university lecturer, and Ontario spokesperson for obsolete social sanities.

RANK AND FILE
The small minority of Trade Unionists who actually vote NDP, for which insolence they are immediately beaten up on by members of the Teamster's Union.

BEER CULTURE AS DATE RAPE
For Molson's huge fly-in-the-beerheads concert in Tuktoyaktuk in 1995, the band *Metallica* reportedly got a million dollars, *Hole* a half a million, while the local community got $35,000 in tarnished loonies and about 35,000 tons of garbage to bury. Anyone who can find a single redeeming element to this genial piece of cultural genocide please contact the United Nations.

RAPTORS
a) birds of prey, like hawks, eagles, owls, highly sensitive to DDT;
b) Toronto pro basketball franchise named after animated Steven Spielberg movie characters. Ten years from now, they'll have to be renamed when some archaeologist dis-

covers that velociraptors actually lived on cream cheese and behaved like barnyard chickens. (This is better than the Vancouver Grizzlies, who are a marketing error: wrong name, wrong city once Vancouver's Hong Kong money evaporates).

RCMP (MOUNTIES)

Originally guys in attractive red suits organized to convince wild Indians that white people are friends of Santa Claus. Now chiefly found standing next to Royal Family members during state visits, dead asleep outside 24 Sussex Drive, or driving around small towns without ever getting out of their cars. The RCMP occasionally become the focus of government inquiries concerning the failure of the force to do anything since 1970 except hire lots of CSIS agents from its own ranks, burn innocent people's barns and foul up major bribe investigations. During the last round of budgetary belt tightening, the Federal government sold the RCMP rights to Walt Disney.

REALISM

Principle widely fondled in the Federal government that supposes that "reality" for Canadians consists of lying on their collective back and letting corporate multinationals or the United States screw them out of their birthrights and their remaining wealth.

REAL ESTATE (formerly land and/or buildings)

Urban doomsday industry created during the 1970s by inducing governments to restrict available development lands so as to artificially inflate land values. Land development companies then ratcheted land values further upward by selling properties to themselves at inflated values and interest rates in order to avoid taxes, thus invoking a volatile financial version of the Chinese Fire Drill in which crazed developers and their bankers chase each other to catch nonexistent assets while they float upward or avoid plummeting properties whenever their real value becomes momentarily visible.

REFORM PARTY

Growing neo-vigilante fringe whose members want to cut taxes, disband the civil service (exterminate it, in extremist quarters), make the poor work harder, and expel all those dark-skinned immigrants so that Canadians can have as little fun as they did in the 1930s. Ultimate goal is to have the Americans walk in and restore order the way they did in Panama and Vietnam.

RED BOOKS

A strange political phenomenon that occurs when the firebugs gain control of the fire hall. E.g., the red-covered collections of Mao Tse-Tung's deep thoughts during the Chinese Cultural Revolution, and the Liberal Party policy books in the 1993 and 1997 Canadian general elections. The book you are reading right now, by contrast, is *not* a red book.

RED TORIES

Red Tories are conservatives who believe in capitalism and in moderate social democratic public policy. Until their extermination in the 1993 federal election, they were the reason that *all* the major parties in the Canadian political spectrum operated in territory slightly to the left of, say, the Clinton Democrats in the U.S. Kim Campbell was, for instance, a fairly typical Red Tory. She'd actually read several pages of 18th Century philosopher Edmund Burke, played a musical instrument, could speak a foreign language and, as justice minister, introduced an amendment to the nation's Human Rights Act to protect the rights of homosexuals. When asked by a member of the Family Values Caucus of her party what in the world she thought she was doing, she replied, "Justice." Other Red Tories of note: Joe Clark, Bob Stanfield and NDP leader Alexis McDonut's current boyfriend.

REFERENDA AND INITIATIVES

Ersatz Americanizing device arising out of constitutional debate in which self-serving choices are offered to citizens by governments wanting to add to their banana collections. In practice, referenda serve to make the rich and aggressive more rich, aggressive and right wing.

RESOURCES

What Canada tries to export, usually in the most unprocessed possible form.

MAURICE RICHARD

Archetypal Québécois, then and now. During the 1950s he was hockey's fastest and most exciting player. Currently working as Jacques Parizeau's body double. "If you try to stop me, I'll break my stick across your forehead, score spectacular goals and blame the English for everything."

DANIEL RICHLER

Rod Stewart look-a-like who can relate equally easily to Robert
Hughes and to people who think they're vampires. That'll make
him a future culture hero and a bridge between the past and
future of Canadian culture—if we're lucky. If we're unlucky,
Richler will simply become another TV-head with a big nose.

MORDECAI RICHLER

Grumpy 1950s-style novelist, fine essayist and better political
commentator who pointed out that Quebec, in its efforts to secure the purity of its indigenous culture and national character,
borders on the same goofy chauvinist excesses that energized
Fascist regimes during the 1930s. Quebec nationalists and their
English-language sympathizers revile Richler with a passion not
seen since the McCarthy era, demonstrating the accuracy of his
claims.

RIR (Real Interest Rate)

The difference between the rate of inflation and the Bank of
Canada's prime lending rate. Across western economies since
1930, the RIR has fluctuated between 1 and 3 percent. In Canada
between 1988 and 1996, the RIR ran between 5 and 8 percent,
thereby providing unreasonably high profits for the bond market and banks. It's down for the 1997 general election, but watch
it climb again in 1998.

LLOYD ROBERTSON

CTV news anchor and "Canada's most trusted voice", the now
ancient Robertson goes off his medication only during Gemini

week and during Federal elections, most of which he spends at the hairdressers, adding yet another hue to his hair. There's still no evidence that he's more than vaguely aware that the disasters he's recounting from the teleprompters have anything to do with living human beings, which until recently was not something he ran into much at CTV's Toronto studios.

SVEND ROBINSON

Gay activist MP and euthanasia enthusiast from B.C. He's also the most intelligent NDP MP since T. C. Douglas, and, given that he's been sent to Ottawa by a working class Vancouver suburb, a man who obviously knows how to run a local constituency. These have been, so far, minor accomplishments. Too bad the NDP didn't have the courage to elect him leader of the party. If it had, the party could have self-destructed in much more interesting and educative ways than it has.

ROC

Damaging acronym carelessly hoisted into public consciousness by English language university professors at Unity conferences attempting to describe all those things that don't have the cachet of Quebec. It means, literally, "rest of Canada". Now, in every ambitious sect and faction around the country, anyone not in the tribal circle is a ROCer.

Well, ROC on, then.

ROCKY MOUNTAINS

Pile of large rocks that take up most of the land area of British Columbia. Beloved of Japanese tourists and forestry multinationals.

Japanese use them for sentimental nature hikes and safe photo-graphic subjects, while the multinationals find that their vari-able landscapes and inaccessibility make it easier to hide the fact that forestry over-harvesting is denuding B.C. trees. The presence of these mountains occasionally gives Albertans living in the vicinity cause to doubt their cherished belief that the world is flat and that semitrailer trucks should be driven over all parts of it with their radios blaring songs about how great Texas is.

TED ROGERS

Cable mogul equally dedicated to the total privatization of Canadian broadcasting as to the total Americanization of Cana-dian television. He's also interested in technology convergence where profitable to him. If anyone can find an original idea, or one with redeeming social value in the vicinity of this man, please contact the CRTC.

ROY ROMANOW

Saskatchewan premier. He isn't T. C. Douglas. On the other hand, he isn't Ralph Klein, either. . . . Or is he?

RRSPS

Now, these are fine things for cautious middle-aged folks, but the amount of bank propaganda aimed at making people in their twenties worry about not having RRSPs when they ought to be out getting drunk, avoiding STDs and generally having a good time is a piece of social engineering that isn't going to help any-one except the banks.

MOSHE SAFDIE

Israeli-Canadian architect who designed Expo 67's leaky residential community, Habitat. Also designed the new Vancouver Public Library, which seems to suggest he's gotten better.

SALMON FISHERY

West Coast equivalent of cod fishery. It is being destroyed by general over-fishing of both salmon and herring stocks, infusion of genetically narrow fish farming, inability to institute sensible pollution control regulations, and the usual infestation of drunk and incompetent fisheries statisticians.

RICK SALUTIN

Grumpy House Communist at the *Globe & Mail*, and Rosedale party animal.

SASKATCHEWAN

Wheat-growing province and birthplace of Canadian social democracy. Along with most of the good ideas that have influenced Canadian politics since 1945, the province is rapidly divesting itself of socialist and grain-farming population in order to become a zone of fast-silting hydroelectric and irrigation projects for the U.S. cornbelt. Only province with perfectly straight borders.

SASKATOON

Canada's most functional and integrated city, and among the few where Biculturalism was taken seriously. About 90 percent of Ottawa's competent bureaucrats are from Saskatoon. Most are bilingual women with red hair.

SATURDAY NIGHT

In the old wintry Canada, Saturday night was for listening to *Hockey Night in Canada* radio broadcasts, for getting drunk and running pickup trucks into snowbanks after one's favourite team won or lost. In the summer Saturday night was also an excuse for a pissup, for punching out one's loved ones, drowning in a boating accident, or all three of those. By the 1990s, Saturday night has become a "winter quality time" period for urbanites, usually spent at expensive restaurants sipping newvo bojoly or as part of all-weekend seminars to hone real estate, investment, or interpersonal skills. Country or *faux* country dwellers spend winter Saturday nights in hospital emergency wards after drunken snowmobiling or skiing accidents.

SATURDAY NIGHT MAGAZINE

Ontario arts journal at one time a major *Atlantic Monthly* wannabe designed to convince Toronto residents that Canada's culture was viable and its writers that magazines could actually pay writers a decent fee for services. Now mostly a *Globe & Mail* advertising flyer written and edited exclusively by people on Conrad Black's cocktail party list.

JOHN RALSTON SAUL

He wears bedroom slippers in public and looks like one of those kids who got beaten up on a lot in elementary and high school, but appearances can be deceiving. He's the only genuine intellectual he-man this country has.

SCARBOROUGH CENTRE: ONTARIO

Plague Mall #4: Canada's answer to the Bronx Zoo.

R. MURRAY SCHAFER

Acoustical educator and Canada's most original and unortho-
dox musical composer. His thirty year project to free serious
music from the concert hall has met with limited success, but
has been a tremendous lot of fun for anyone he's involved in it.
Schafer's sub-project is getting people to do whatever it is they
can't possibly do, at which his success rate is astounding. He
despises pianos, which explains why he was the first recipient of
the Glenn Gould prize.

BARBARA ANN SCOTT

Does anyone other than television figure skating commentators
remember who Barbara Ann Scott was and did? She's what
Grace Kelly would have been like if she'd spent her life in a
pickle jar instead of marrying a prince.

DONNA SCOTT

Current Canada Council CEO whose view of the arts, as stated
in the 1995-96, is that they "boost exports" and are useful to
the tourism industry. Anyone who has ever seen Scott elbow
her way to a bar wishes she were more interested in art and
artists, less in demonstrating how much fun survival of the fittest
can be and a lot less determined to harmonize Canada Council
programs with those of the Business Council on National
Issues.

SEAL PUP HARVEST

A sore point for hungry Newfoundlanders, who know that the cod stocks ain't coming back so long as the eastern seaboard remains overpopulated with seals being personally chaperoned to lunch and dinner by middle class econightmares in yachts. If only chickens and our domestic poor were as picturesque as baby seals. . . .

THE SECRET WAR

Ongoing in Canada since 1979 between Bond/Banking Sector (BBS) and Real Estate Sector. Unrealistic real estate profits depend on high rates of inflation and stable Real Interest Rates (see RIR), while inordinate BBS profits depend on low inflation and high RIR. Until 1988, Real Estate did very well. Since then, BBS has won every battle, which is why most of Canada's major real estate developers have quietly disappeared into bankruptcy and the smaller ones *all* changed the names of their companies between 1988 and 1991.

THE SENATE

Vestigial British institution originally designed to protect traditional property rights and privileges from the belligerent, ill-bred pigs in Parliament. In Canadian practice, it has become a pasture for elderly belligerent, ill-bred parliamentary pigs. Recent governments, while making grunting noises to the public about disbanding the Senate, have turned it into a partisan institution with powers parallel to those of Parliament. This alteration will paralyze both bodies, leaving power in the hands of the prime minister and his close friends, along with the U.S. State Department and Trade Secretariat.

SEPARATISM

Popular movement in Quebec and Alberta aimed at forming right wing republics under the political and cultural guidance of France or the United States. Separatism began in Quebec as a social democratic movement designed to invert traditional domination by anglophone Canadian business interests. In Alberta, the sources of the movement can be traced back to a long-standing wish of Albertans to reify creationist theories, along with absolute enforcement of missionary positions in social and sexual politics.

THE GROUP OF SEVEN

The kindest way to look at this group of outdoorsmen, cocksmen, poor swimmers, drunks and socialites is to call them the visual arts equivalent of Don Messer's *Jubilee*. But as the official CanCon sector of Canadian visual arts shrinks to a three mile radius around Kleinburg, Ontario, can't the rest of us admit that Harold Town and Greg Curnoe, along with a half dozen others who are still alive, are superior art guys in every possible way?

JACK SHADBOLT

Elderly West Coast transcultural thief and self-promoter who once imagined, in public, that the future would see everyone owning their own sailboat with a famous painter's work on the mainsail. He intended to paint his own sail but the project was shelved due to the late 20th Century.

SHAW FESTIVAL

Niagara-on-the-Lake tourist sanctuary and opportunity to sell pot-pourris and other smelly foreign-made semi-crafts to those with poor-to-neutral tastes.

SHIELD, THE CANADIAN

Semi-circular rock formation surrounding central Canada mistakenly believed by many Canadians to be a legitimate defence against Soviet missile attacks and U.S. cultural, economic and military invasions. In the 1990s, the formation is proving to be a corralling zone for incoming U.S. and globalist economic and cultural roundup/exterminations of indigenous behaviours.

ROSEANNE SKOKE

Nova Scotia Member of Parliament and the Daffy Duck of the 35th Canadian Parliament. It would have been fun to see her debate with Don Blenkarn, the Elmer Fudd of the Mulroney years, and more fun still to watch her fly in formation with the Reform party's MPs. Alas, she was defeated in the 1997 Liberal party wipeout in the Maritimes as proof to Jean Chrétien that every cloud has a silver lining.

SKYTRAIN

Greater Vancouver's public transit system is an international transit joke. It works on the same principle as a Lionel toy train, the cars have roughly the same capacity as a London taxi, and the opening day per-ride operating subsidy was about $6. Why did this happen? Well, when the local planners came up with conventional Light Rail transit in 1980, then-Municipal Affairs minister Bill Vander Zalm told his people to find him another technology. They found ALRT: $400 million more to build, half the capacity, but they didn't have to pay any uppity bus drivers to run the trains. The teen gangs love it, international transit experts still have the giggles and the per-ride subsidy, with inflation is up around $18 a ride.

JOEY SMALLWOOD

Folk historian, anecdotalist, character, first premier of Newfoundland. Newfoundland politics hasn't ever gotten over him, given the parade of latter-day Joeys who have followed him into the office. See *Frank Moores, Brian Tobin*

SNOW

A substance used for scenery and skiing enhancement. Typical flavours are corn, powder, fresh and yellow, the latter of which is a future export item to the United States. Snow is illegal on flat surfaces in Quebec, where it is replaced with copious amounts of salt whenever those filthy English Canadian pigs in the Federal government tamper with the weather and cause it to snow on native French speakers.

SOCIAL CREDIT

Canadian sociopolitical movement centred mostly in Western Canada. Originally grounded in the biblical prohibition against usury, and turn-of-the-century economic and social theories of Major Douglas that suggest that monetary supply should be determined by productivity rather than by thieves, hysterics and morons. Out of that sometimes sensible ground has grown a series of xenophobic right wing political movements that want to shoot the poor, ethnics, trade unionists, educated people and anyone else who doesn't desperately want to own a Cadillac. (See W.A.C. Bennett, Ernest and Preston Manning, the Reform Party, APEC and large elements of the post-Levesque Parti Québécois.)

SPEAKER'S CORNER

Toronto Queen Street demographic technofacility in which culturally distressed or distraught individuals seek loved ones, complain about personal problems and the government, or crowd together in groups to make smartass remarks and sing badly enough to humiliate themselves. There are those in the media who see this as a relevant form of contemporary democracy, while others wonder what making an ass of oneself on television has to do with anything.

SOMALIA INQUIRY

Ottawa finger-pointing rave that illustrates just how powerful Canada's military bureaucracy really is. The military mavens have been able to stonewall numerous ambitious ministers, the prime minister and the media with ease. You want this mess sorted out? Fire them all on the grounds that they're either corrupt or incompetent and therefore shouldn't be permitted to carry firearms. Or, donate them all to Somalia, a country that appears to like armed gangs.

EVAN SOLOMAN

Personably articulate editor of *Shift* magazine, which began as one of those suicidally well-intentioned literary journals Canada produces too many of and has lately become an instrument of pop/technology culture almost as silly and pompous in its inflations as *Wired* magazine. Soloman is in serious danger of becoming the youngest good old boy in Canada, but to his credit, he isn't about to become another SuperMind.

SOUTHAM

Family of seventeen pudgy, WASP dailies that were blowing in the wind until Conrad Black got hold of them.

SQUEEGEE KIDS

Youth culture's way of letting the rest of us know that for anyone under twenty-five, this is now a Third World country. The responses to these kids from older and wealthier elements of the community sometimes appear to be guided by the Mexican government, other times by the Three Stooges.

BLACK SQUIRRELS

European ecovermin spreading from major urban centres to eradicate our smaller native red squirrels. Just be thankful nobody thought to introduce hyenas into our urban parkland.

TORONTO STAR

Canada's best newspaper, recently slimmed down and brought far too close to tabloid journalism's style-book for anyone's comfort except TorStar's accountants.

STEVE STAVRO

Shirt-maker, owner of the Toronto Maple Leafs, possible Harold Ballard impersonator who was smart enough to hire Ken Dryden as club president but might not be smart enough to let him do his job.

HOWARD STERN

Supposed threat to civilization. It is hard to get upset about a man Canada's humourless safety Nazis and Quebec sovereigntists agree is a threat to everything they hold sacred and unassailable. Stern may not be running Mordecai Richler's New York bureau, but he's more fun than our own home-based open mouth radio bigots. The CRTC's CanCon regulations weren't meant to protect us from people like Howard Stern. They were created to keep our airways from being filled with market researchers demographic sludge programmed in some Muzak megafactory in Ohio. Any anyway, maybe we should be less concerned about protecting ourselves from sacred cow-slaughtering ego-puncturing radio goofballs and more worried about who'll protect us from the people who think we need to be protected from the goofballs.

ELVIS STOJKO

Brilliant, innovative miniature figure skater. There must be something fundamentally good about a country where someone like Stojko isn't forced to drive a forklift for a living. Generally considered way too heterosexual by some of his colleagues, who think his idea of "artistic expression" too much resembles a fisting gesture reminiscent of a gay S&M bathhouse nightmare.

STRATFORD FESTIVAL

One of Canada's tourist jewels, probably an amethyst and definitely semi-precious. Now that the government is disappearing, some say the festival is being held together by a facade of brassy pretension, pomposity and a municipal tourist scheme to open a graveyard for famous actors.

STRUCTURAL ADJUSTMENT

Econopolitical ideological device originally developed by IMF/World Bank for use in bankrupt Third World countries. The device diverts national and personal incomes and productivity to pay off debts incurred by corrupt government officials as foreign aid. It was supposedly meant to finance loony Western-style industrial megaprojects, but was actually spent on arming militias and providing luxury autos and villas for officials, their families and political allies. The invariable result of Structural Adjustment is elevated prices for essentials, collapse of social services and increased income gaps. Now being applied to industrialized countries, including Canada.

SUN

Loosely affiliated chain of five daily red-neck tabloids noted for *faux* cheese-and-beef-cake photos, stratospheric right-wing columnists, and stripper-show ads. Not to be confused with heavenly orbs or the Vancouver *Sun*, which is a Southam paper edited by ex-staffers from the *Globe & Mail*. The *Sun* chain also owns and runs the *Financial Post* out of its Toronto office. If you're ever in need of a cheap laugh while in downtown Toronto, try sitting in the joint reception area of these two papers and guessing who works for which paper—and what the differences in spiritual affiliation are.

SUDBURY

Moonscape created by nickel mining debris made this mid-Ontario disaster the ecological equivalent of hell. It is now being recycled by the film industry as a prime set for post-nuclear holocaust science fiction flicks.

SUPERMINDS

Corporate term for intellectuals able to frame visible trends, generalized themes and occasionally serious ideas in terms vague enough to appeal to business executives and government leaders at luncheons and seminars. Canada has a longstanding tradition of Superminds stretching back to Harold Innis and Marshall McLuhan. Pierre Trudeau, incidentally, wanted to be one.

DERRICK DE KERCKHOVE

Techno-enthusiast, gabber, corporate rah-rah machine, tenth-rate Marshall McLuhan. He'd like to believe he's Canada's answer to MIT Media Lab's Nicolas Negroponte, with whom he shares the thrill of never having met a question without a shallow answer.

ARTHUR KROKER

Michel Foucault meets *Wired* magazine. Any more than five of this man's sentences in a row will give even the most open-minded people nuke-level migraine headaches.

FRANK OGDEN

Vancouver futurist and general media aide-de-camp. Yeah, sure, Frank. Life in Canada probably *would* be better if everyone owned a Pentium-based PC and five grand worth of other communications technology. But the big monitors and minitowers don't fit into a shopping cart, and the Pentium processor has a tendency to crash when you're trying to be interactive from a cardboard shelter in a mall parking lot in a snowstorm.

BRUCE POWE

A likeable man who began well with a serious book entitled *The Solitary Outlaw*, Powe once appeared likely to become McLuhan's true heir, but now seems more determined to rewrite Pierre Berton's *The Comfortable Pew* for the remaining listeners of Morningside and otherwise drown all sense in metaphoric drooling over electronic communications. A big fave of Pierre Trudeau in his dotage, an endorsement which may or may not be a compliment.

DAVID SUZUKI

Science writer, popularizing ecologist, fruit fly vivisectionist and television host. A lot of people dislike Suzuki for his arrogance and single-mindedness, but whatever style problems he has, he's the only science-based intellectual in the country trying to integrate long-range ecological planning with contingency and common sense. (Sorry, but Jay Ingram isn't an intellectual. He's a television host.)

SWARMINGS

Okay all you adults out there. It's getting so you can't take public transit or go to the mall without being afraid that a gang of angry, crazy teenagers is going to swarm you and steal your money, right? But before we toss them all in the slammer, let's take a deep breath and ask ourselves why they're angry, and what's making them crazy.

ATHABASKA TAR SANDS

Hey! Isn't Alberta the province that has squealed the most hysterically about government intervention sullying the entrepreneurial *élan* of the private sector? So how come it also has allowed untold millions in government subsidies to be sunk into a cockeyed scheme to extract oil from its icy northern sands to pump into a marketplace that demonstrably doesn't want it. Along with Peter Pocklington, who's had a money hose stuck in the side of the Alberta government treasury for twenty years now, it kind of makes you wonder what they're really squealing about. . . .

TELEFILM CANADA

Primary funding agency for Canadian film production. After a childhood and adolescence marked by alternately courageous and foolhardy decisions, TeleFilm has devolved into a bottom-lining bureaucracy most likely to offer funding to Can/Am co-productions using Canadian bit actors and technical crews, American lead actors, post production and profits. Isn't likely to be funding any films like *Trainspotting* in the foreseeable future.

TELEVISION INDUSTRY SPOKESPERSONS

a) accountants armed with the latest Neilsen ratings announcing that in the free market system, the public has a right to the kind of programming it demands;

b) well-dressed persons announcing corporate media mergers; or

c) government ministers and their stooges announcing public sector cutbacks and programming cancellations. All three of these definitions will be valid until well after the year 2000, or until the disappearance of public broadcasting.

TEMAGAMI

Large area in Northern Ontario once filled with white pine and now a battle zone for environmentalists, loggers and tourist camp owners sucking up to the outdoor recreation market. At issue is a 1400 hectare stand of old growth white pine, one of the last in North America, and more significant but less glamourous than B.C.'s tiny Karmanah Valley.

VERONICA TENNANT

Toronto socialite and culture diva. Recently acted as front-person for cable arts network that would have catered exclusively to the tastes of Toronto Symphony Orchestra subscribers and other *aficionados* of formal wear.

THANKSGIVING

Mid-October harvest festival where we're supposed to thank God we're not Americans. So far, so good.

MARGO TIMMINS

Esquire magazine decided that Timmins was a world class babe a few years ago, and Canadians have been paying for it ever since. It would be interesting to find out whether she can hold her key when she's off the antidepressants.

BRIAN TOBIN

Federal Fisheries minister during the 1995 Turbot Wars with Spain, and current premier of Newfoundland. A Great Communicator, whatever that means aside from giving the media good clips and an occasional bloodless naval battle. Too bad Newfoundland doesn't have its own navy. Don't expect Tobin to dance the way Clyde Wells did.

TOPLESS LAWS

A couple of years ago a university of Waterloo student named Gwen Jacobs got annoyed after the police charged her for walking around with her T-shirt off. She went to court and won Canadian women the right to go topless whenever and wherever they want. While the guys down at the bar are waiting for the topless ruling to become a compulsory rule, a lot of women are waking up to the fact that rights need to have a basis in common custom, imagination and maybe common sense before they've really been won.

TORONTO

Once among the dullest cities on the planet, and for a few years during the 1970s and 80s, among the most self-proud. Toronto has become a great city by taking in more than a million immigrants in the last two decades and becoming multicultural and multiracial without becoming violent. In the 1980s, the global economy kicked the city so hard that it forgot about being world class, and its citizens became kinder and more cosmopolitan. It is now—and without dispute—the largest safe city in the world. It has a thousand small, often exotic neighbourhoods, and outside of its financial district, appears to be a deciduous forest when you fly over it in a plane. Toronto is currently under siege by right wing suburbanites wanting to rid it of immigrants or any other kind of complex human textures, and by left wing anti-smoking and safety zealots similarly overeager to supervise the city's uniquely liberal quality of life.

TORSTAR

It's a neat-sounding name for a news service, but it's really a bottom-liner's device for exterminating local coverage. Owns and is presumably responsible for Harlequin Books.

TRADE BALANCE

Multipurpose monetarist indicator that
a) propagandizes gross import/export balance as a meaning- ful indication of economic health, which it is not;
b) simplifies and distorts the nature of international eco- nomic behaviors;
c) disables the common sense of everyone credulous enough not to question its validity as a commercial indicator.

TRADE DEFICIT

An economic condition easily confused with public deficits, and therefore highly useful to New Conservatives wanting to convince everyone that social services are superfluous and communistic. Over the last twenty years the United States has had a trade deficit equal in dollar value to the combined assets of the Third World, while Canada has maintained a trade surplus. Anybody see any profound differences between the two economies, not counting the greater percentage of homeless people in the U.S.?

TRADE SURPLUS

Canada has a large and chronic trade surplus that tends to widen whenever unemployment jumps. Doesn't this suggest that a trade surplus is a pipeline of brown bovine by-product injected directly into our collective brain? See *current account balance*

TRANS-CANADA HIGHWAY

Pre-1960s device to unify the country and foster real estate development and population growth along coherent corridors. Like the CPR in the 1870s, the TCH mainly benefitted the contractors who built it, and made it possible for the rest of us to go nowhere faster. By the 1980s the highway was heavily populated by challenged persons hopping from coast to coast and other publicity stunts that amused the rest of the world but influenced Quebec's separatists not one iota.

TREES

Canada was once covered with trees, but fifty years of treating them as a renewable resource to be renewed only where clearcuts are visible to tourists from main highways has left vast tracts of the country as denuded neo-tundra. In water-rich B.C. and parts of Northern Alberta, Manitoba and Ontario, this appears to be a subconscious form of reservoir preparation.

MICHEL TREMBLAY

Slightly over-the-hill Quebec playwright who wrote a drama about a drag queen and a homosexual motorcyclist titled *Hosanna* about thirty years ago, which revived live theatre in Canada/Quebec. Since then, Quebec has produced more homosexual plays per capita than any other jurisdiction on the planet.

LEON TROTSKY

Famed Communist dissident sighted in Nova Scotia in the 1930s by Timothy Findley. Trotsky is still rumoured to control Canada's postal unions, even though he died in 1940 in Mexico from an ice-pick in the back of his head.

FLYING TRUCK WHEELS

We deregulate the trucking industry and let American truckers weaken our indigenous truckers with unfair competition that leave the truckers unable to afford proper vehicle maintenance. Then when the wheels start to fly off their vehicles and kill people, we blame it on the truckers and feel righteous about running harassing safety checks that regularly take away the trucker's livelihoods. I mean, geez, guys. If we really want *laissez-faire* capitalism, we can't start whining just because a few truck tires whistle by our heads once in a while. . . .

MARGARET TRUDEAU

Daughter of St. Laurent-era federal cabinet minister James Sinclair, she married Pierre Trudeau at age twenty-two, bore three children, refused to wear panties while in New York City, and was generally the same sort of political asset as Mackenzie King's cocker spaniel. Self-appointed disciple of English poet William Blake and chronic perpetrator of similar desecrations. Still, there'll be an awful lot of aging males who'll breathe a sigh of relief when she finally loses her looks.

PIERRE ELLIOTT TRUDEAU

Jesuit, acrobat, and Canadian prime minister 1968-84 (with short breaks) and a current object of nostalgia as the last Canadian political leader with a connected brain and spinal cord. It'll be fifty years before it's clear whether he was a great statesman or a blundering egomaniac who poisoned the country permanently by repatriating the constitution. But he sure had a lot more style than the men who've followed him.

TRUST COMPANIES

Canadian version of U.S. Savings and Loans, and nearly as prone to bankruptcy. Canadian trust companies tend to be larger than their American counterparts, and are sometimes barely disguised subsidiaries of charter banks who use them as repositories for their high risk loans. Trust companies are the last people sensible folks should trust with their money, but if you're investing someone else's, what the hell? Canada's trust companies are rumoured to be nearing completion of a twenty-year talent hunt for the next Nick Leeson.

THE TURBOT WAR

Alright, let's go over this one more time. We boarded a couple of Spanish fishing boats, defeated the Spanish Armada, turned Brian Tobin into a culture hero, and gave Newfoundlanders a real reason to go out, get drunk and celebrate. But was it really a great naval victory? Is it going to save the east coast fishery?

JOHN TURNER

Whitest-of-the-white prime minister for a few months after Pierre Trudeau saw the writing on the wall. Turner quietly travelled the country and listened to nearly every sector of the political spectrum before the 1988 election. He turned out to be the only political figure in the country who understood the implications of Mulroney's free trade initiatives, and came close to saving the country from what it is today. Unfortunately, he was also a bum-pinching Good Old Boy who had trouble staying on his feet in a social breeze. We'll never know if he was the right man at the wrong time, or the wrong man at the right time. Wife Giels, who was the best qualified PM's wife in a half-century, apparently has a discreet opinion about this.

SHANIA TWAIN

Faux First Nations country singer whose singing career is being jeopardized by the suspicion, created by her wardrobe and her music videos, that her ankles are about the same circumference as her waist.

UKRAINE, THE

Don't let this go to your head, but a recent survey indicates that citizens of the Ukraine find Canadians "sexy".

UNION MEMBERS

Elderly workers identifiable by the amount of recreational technology parked in their garages, and by the fact that they're overweight and leaning toward the Reform Party. Why would anyone under thirty join a trade union in the 1990s?

UNIVERSITY PROFESSORS, TENURED

The last outpost of delusional Marxist optimism left in Western civilization. Aside from the tiny minority of scholars, university teachers and intellectuals and a slightly larger underclass of sessional instructors who simply teach classes and scramble for wages, Canadian universities have become a zone of educational and intellectual misrule, populated by Stalinoid cranks of all political persuasions trying to decide whether it's more important to impose a Dictatorship of the Correct, have free dental care for tenured faculty or ensure that faculty offspring be able to study both classical and modern ballet. Nobody, meanwhile, is getting much of a university education in the sense that Cardinal Newman intended, and the universities aren't exactly cranking out better citizens. On the other hand, does anyone out there want to shut the universities down so we can go with television and/or the aggressive ignorance that are our only apparent alternatives?

UPPER CANADA COLLEGE

If you don't believe Canada has a class system, check the number of political, corporate and cultural Visigoths who graduated from this ivy-clad downtown Toronto factory for closet homosexuals and industrial dominatrixes.

JACK VALENTI

The devil behind the U.S. film industry. Jack Valenti ordered Brian Mulroney to attend a meeting with him near the end of negotiatory process of the Canada/U.S. Free Trade Agreement to explain just exactly why Canada needed an independent culture. During the meeting, Valenti supposedly slapped Mulroney around the room until the awed P.M. began to weep, after which Valenti dictated the wording of the alleged cultural exemption that has put Canada's cultural industries, along with much of its media and communications sector into a freefall that will end in total offshore or Conrad Black-type control.

VANCOUVER

Picturesque settlement of about 180,000 wealthy WASPs and recent Asian immigrant entrepreneurs, usually found carrying cellular phones and wanking on about being World Class. Greater Vancouver contains eleven separate climates not found elsewhere in Canada, all of which are characterized by thick moss cover, and the unshakable feeling that you're trapped in an episode of the X Files.

VICTORIA

The last functioning outpost of the British Empire and alleged seat of alleged B.C. government. Famous for untreated sewage outfalls that make local beaches about as safe and pleasant for swimming as your toilet. Such problems are, somehow, undetectable during High Tea at the Empress Hotel.

VIMY RIDGE
One of Canada's genuine moments of national glory, and a long, long way from Somalia.

MICHAEL WALKER
Aggrieved White Guy and Fraser Institute majordomo whose economic and political views are gospel within the Reform Party. Tends to froth at the mouth and write in megasyllabic Matthew Arnold prose whenever his word is not taken at face value.

PAMELA WALLIN
Television journalist who lost a battle of egos to Peter Mansbridge and found herself broadcasting interviews from a studio that appears to be in a spaceship. Her interview with Toronto basketball player Damon Stoudamire was arguably the silliest interview with a black public figure since Barbara Frum interviewed Nelson Mandela. Wallin's journalistic reputation has been elevated by the ascension of Hana Gartner to her old job.

WAL-MART
The unofficial church of American merchandise coming to your community soon, if it hasn't already. Wal-Mart is the truest reflection of our future in the global economy and NAFTA: American management, minimum-wage Canadian clerks, and products manufactured in Mexico.

WATER

By 2010, fresh water will be Canada's chief natural resource. Most of it will be shipped to the U.S. to slake the thirst of California's lawns, or to other points in the U.S. south to flush out the industrial machinery shipped from Ontario and the U.S. Northeast.

WAYNE AND SHUSTER

Leslie Neilsen brushing his teeth without a camera on him is funnier than the entire career of these two *Happy Gang* refugees.

ANDREW LLOYD WEBER

The limits of Canada's market-oriented cultural imagination as conceived by Garth Drabinsky.

WEEKLIES

An industry once mostly locally-owned and written, now almost wholly controlled by newspaper chains, who have destaffed them editorially in search of enhanced profits. The sole exception to this appears to be Toronto's TorStar-owned but highly entertaining *Eye Weekly*, the entertainment paper for people under forty who wear leather jackets, drink beer and have tattoos. See *independent weeklies*

WESTMOUNT

Montreal shopping district and English-language lifestyle zone. Designated a French language and politics-free shopping sanctuary by Mila Mulroney and co-members of Montreal's International Shopping Team during the 1980s.

HILARY WESTON

Former Irish mannequin, now a Toronto socialite who married, uh, well. Her appointment as Ontario's lieutenant governor appears to be Michael Harris' sop to the former ruling class of the province. Weston's only obvious qualification for the job is her talent for arriving late at formal events and then leaving early.

WEWAPs

White ethnics with attitude problems. They're the country's least recognized hope for a better — or at least more interesting — future.

BOB WHITE

Head of the Canadian Labour Congress, whether he's holding the post of president or not. He led Canada's auto workers out of the corrupt American United Auto Workers Union, and became the model for a series of similar Canadian union liberations. Avoided becoming leader of federal NDP by sheer force of character and remains the only over-thirty-five trade unionist in Canada with a waist size below thirty-six inches.

RUDY WIEBE

Alberta author, self-promoter, cultural appropriator and bore. Not to draw conclusions from circumstantial evidence, but an astonishingly high percentage of Alberta residents are in favour of ending public support for the arts.

WINNIPEG

Too hot in summer, too cold in winter, and too subject to spring floods to do much more than be envious of Minneapolis.

Loreena McKennitt does well here, and so does the Guess Who, the Crash Test Dummies, and other embarrassments. Winnipeg's primary cultural amenities include the Golden Boy statue, Kaleki's fries, and the banking temples that have turned the centre of Canada at Portage and Main into a dead zone. Don't miss any of these.

GIZELLA WITKOWSKY

Prima ballerina of National Ballet forced into retirement because she looks like she's seen life inside a trailer-park and says "Fuck you" at cocktail parties. Doesn't front for television networks and wasn't offered a farewell tour.

GEORGE WOODCOCK

UBC academic, friend of George Orwell, author of sixty-four books, who died in 1995. Woodcock was a cross between Harold Innis and Hammond Innes, but less interesting than either. Watch for a deluge of largely uncritical biographies to follow in the next five years, all written as turgidly as he wrote his own books.

WORKING CLASS

Former "revolutionary" class now virtually extinct, both politically and genetically. Replaced during the 1980s by "ordinary working Canadians" who are now fast becoming as hard to find as members of the revolutionary working class and/or the proletariat.

WORLD CLASS

Real estate buzzword to describe the inclusion to existing infrastructure of chronic high unemployment, urban transportation gridlock, derelict industrial sites, empty office buildings, rental inflation, high crime levels, food banks and people living in cardboard boxes.

WRITERS UNION OF CANADA

A not-quite-union of mainly over-forty writers who desperately want to be professionals, more desperately want to curry favour with aggressive minorities and indifferent governments, but can't quite bring any of it off. So the members dream about having a writers' dental plan, the Union bulks up with children's writers, whines about government cuts, and insists that it can't happen here—and together degenerate into the Canadian Authors Association and yet another group of futile little old men and fuddy-duddy ladies wearing shoes too sensible to have a real imagination riding atop them.

NEIL YOUNG

Canada's finest song-writer—and worst vocalist since Charlie Chamberlain. His father is Scott Young, which makes Neil a second generation cultural treasure.

THE YOUNG

A rapidly aging segment of the Canadian population born between 1950 and 1970 and educated to form a disaffected lumpen bourgeoisie. Presently being heavily propagandized by the right, as are those born after 1970, most of whom are too frightened and angry about their financial futures to be young. See *human resources*

YUGOSLAVIA

The direction in which Canada appears to be heading.

YUKON GOLD

A recently developed species of potato that is tastier than any other, grows better in Canada's climates than in the U.S. It is much more likely to bring down NAFTA and the Canada-U.S. FTA than either Patrick Buchanan or the NDP.

ZEN MASTERS OF BIG BUSINESS:
(THOSE WHO KNOW DON'T SPEAK,
THOSE WHO SPEAK GET LIBEL-CHILLED.)

Black, Bronfman, Irving, McCain, Reichman, Thomson.

MOSES ZNAIMER

Montreal-born Toronto communications mogul and minor movie actor famous for putting his own name in the same typeface as Susan Sarandon and Burt Lancaster when his Toronto television station runs *Atlantic City*. One of many McLuhanites who've never read McLuhan, he's fond of reading on-air from cue cards that predict the death of print. And incidentally, is there anything *revolutionary* about having your news-readers wander around the studio while they read the news?

One last thing. What does it mean when the leader of the revolution wears a ponytail made up exclusively of neck hairs?

THE
DISBELIEVER'S
DICTIONARY

GARFINKLE ESTATE